30 Day Pray For Your Spouse Challenge

Kimberly Moses

Copyright © 2021 by **Kimberly Moses**

All rights reserved. No part of this publication may be reproduced, distributed or transmitted in any form or by any means, including photocopying, recording, or other electronic or mechanical methods, without the prior written permission of the publisher, except in the case of brief quotations embodied in critical reviews and certain other noncommercial uses permitted by copyright law. For permission requests, write to the publisher, addressed "Attention: Permissions Coordinator," at the address below.

Kimberly Moses/Rejoice Essential Publishing

PO BOX 512

Effingham, SC 29541

www.republishing.org

Unless otherwise indicated, scripture is taken from the King James Version.'

Scripture taken from the New King James Version®. Copyright © 1982 by Thomas Nelson. Used by permission. All rights reserved.

30 Day Pray For Your Spouse Challenge/ Kimberly Moses

ISBN-13: 978-1-952312-78-6

LCCN: 2021940595

Dedication

This book wouldn't be possible without the inspiration of the Holy Spirit. Marriage is work and a lifetime commitment. God can restore marriages that seem hopeless. I dedicate this book to those who are believing God to heal their marriage.

2 Timothy 3:16-17 says, "All scripture is given by inspiration of God, and is profitable for doctrine, for reproof, for correction, for instruction in righteousness: That the man of God may be perfect, thoroughly furnished unto all good works."

Table of Contents

INTRODUCTION		1
DAY ONE:	Kindness	7
DAY TWO:	Loving	13
DAY THREE:	No Selfishness	18
DAY FOUR:	Provider	23
DAY FIVE:	Protector	29
DAY SIX:	Friend	35
DAY SEVEN:	Priority	40
DAY EIGHT:	Understanding	46
DAY NINE:	Great Listener	51
DAY TEN:	Great Communication	56
DAY ELEVEN:	Patience	62
DAY TWELVE:	Forgiving	68
DAY THIRTEEN:	Encourager	74
DAY FOURTEEN:	Supporter	80
DAY FIFTEEN:	Companion	85
DAY SIXTEEN:	Spiritual	90
DAY SEVENTEEN:	Healthy	96
DAY EIGHTEEN:	Peaceful	102
DAY NINETEEN:	Great Leader	108
DAY TWENTY:	Go-getter	113
DAY TWENTY ONE:	Trusting	118
DAY TWENTY TWO:	Faithful	123
DAY TWENTY THREE:	Committed	128
DAY TWENTY FOUR:	Right Alignment with God	133
DAY TWENTY FIVE:	Humble	138
DAY TWENTY SIX:	Wisdom	143

DAY TWENTY SEVEN:	Trail Blazer.................................148
DAY TWENTY EIGHT	Confident...................................153
DAY TWENTY NINE:	Debt Free...................................159
DAY THIRTY:	Mentally Stable........................164
ABOUT THE AUTHOR	169

Introduction

Do you want to walk away from your marriage because things got tough? Perhaps you felt you made a mistake and married the wrong person. No matter how you feel, you must do your part and pray for your spouse. When was the last time you covered your spouse in prayer? Surprisingly, some people don't pray at all for their spouse and when they do, their prayers are self-centered. They pray with a motive and use manipulative tactics to control their spouses. God looks at our heart and won't honor "witchcraft" prayers. We can't pray, "Lord, hurt my spouse because they hurt me. Make them pay and suffer." Instead, we have to pray, "Lord, bless my spouse and prosper them," even when they hurt us. We must pray God's blessings upon them when they irritate us. Why? Because we made a vow in God's sight to love our spouse through thick and thin. All relationships have ups and downs. As couples go through challenges, their bond gets stronger if they stick it out. It's easy to walk away when things are hard. However, God can strengthen and bless us if we can stand in faith. As you pray for your spouse, you are loving, serving, and protecting them. You are also fighting for your marriage.

Many times, I wanted to throw in the towel and God spoke to me. He always instructed me to pray for my husband. One day in prayer, He challenged me to pray for my husband for thirty days. I remember making tally marks in my journal and seeing things get better in my home. My husband isn't a bad person, but there are areas for improvement. I'm pretty sure you can relate because we all have room to grow. Every day, God shows us issues in our lives that we need to be delivered from or be transformed into the image of Jesus in a greater measure. For instance, I went to God complaining one day about something my husband had done. Then I heard the Holy Spirit speak, "What about the time you did that?" Immediately, I felt conviction, so I repented.

I decided to always pray for my spouse because that's what I signed up for when I said, "I do." It's my job as a wife to cover my husband in prayer. I am his prophet and intercessor. As a woman, I control the atmosphere in my home because I'm a gatekeeper. I will not allow the enemy to win by stepping over the threshold of the Moses' home. As a minister, I devoted my life to serve others and my husband needs my prayers. It's amazing to see the favor upon his business as I intercede. I'm blown away by how the Lord protects him and I know it's because I'm always lifting him up in prayer. Regardless of what is going on, we must pray because there is a lot at stake. People need you and your spouse to make it. Will you allow your marriage to be a Kingdom example?

Introduction

Perhaps, you are on fire for God and your spouse isn't. Keep loving them because love endures all things. You can win over your spouse with your godly conduct. Since you love them, you must pray for them, especially if they are underneath demonic influence. The enemy might be whispering lies to your spouse and it's up to you to combat it in prayer. A part of loving your spouse is wanting the best for them. Your prayers will make a difference in their life. Even if you don't see the results right now, don't give up because one day you will. Love is an action word. One day, your spouse will thank you for praying for them when they couldn't pray for themselves or when they were in error.

It's so easy to argue and become offended. Yet, you are a child of God and your life isn't your own, so you must serve. Wake up early and bring your spouse before God. Mention their name in the middle of the day. Lastly, pray for them before bed. Prayer does change things. Be patient and wait on the Lord. Sometimes your spouse might not know what's best so take it before God. Only God can rip the stubbornness and pride away. He knows how to transform a hard heart because He is the potter and we are the clay. When you are a servant, you push your feelings to the side and do what's required. Will you serve your spouse in prayer?

Another dimension of praying for your spouse is protecting the blessing of the Lord. Your spouse is a gift. Remember when you were lonely and praying for a mate? Now they are here, so be a good steward over your marriage and cast out the devil. You must pray when things are going well and in the chaos. You must pray a hedge of protection and a wall of fire around your home. Your prayers are more powerful than you think. You might feel things are getting worse since you started praying. It's because the enemy loves to stay hidden and your prayers are causing him to manifest. Your prayers are being the enemy to the surface. Now when the enemy is exposed, use your authority in Jesus, and cast out the spirit.

Since you picked up this book, it's a sign that you want to fight for your marriage. God never gave up on you, so don't give up on your spouse. Jesus even prayed for His crucifiers or the people who hurt him. Can you pass the test and pray for your spouse even when they hurt you? Can you fight for your marriage even when it seems like there is no hope? Everything worth having is worth fighting for. Recognize that you are wrestling against a spirit and it's no match for Jesus Christ. Contend for your marriage and take this 30-day challenge.

As I went into prayer, the Holy Spirit gave me thirty topics to pray for my spouse. I took this assignment on the noon prayer call and others were blessed as well. Let's read a few testimonies.

> *I can say that I see God moving and working on my husband. My husband and I have been separated for four years due to his infidelity and me leaving him. For the first time, since separated, he said that our marriage is worth fighting for, he wants his marriage, and that he loves me last week. He sends daily good morning texts now. We are now communicating without arguing. Also, disagreements are being talked through without anger. He is not carrying the disagreements or anger over to the next day as previously.*

Introduction

He can now sit in the same room with me, watch tv together on the same sofa, and eat and drink together. It's a slow process, but I thank God for every moment of it. Only God... thank you, Lord!!—Metrice Coleman Wilder

I'm not married yet, but I have been praying these declarations every day over my future husband, covering him in prayer and intercession. This was phenomenal and shouldn't be a challenge but an everyday decision to declare favor over your husband. – Amy Cassels

I can honestly say that I gradually see a lot of changes spiritually in my boyfriend. Where there were questions and dry areas, I see God's emphasis and stretching him in places that he thought he couldn't expand on. So please continue the prayer. I actually declare those things over him.—Tiara Figueroa

God taught me to stay the same in my marriage. He encouraged me to continue doing the things I was regularly doing, and not to stop when times get rough. As I obeyed I would see a change in my husband's response towards me. My husband would never text me back. I stayed the same. I continued to respect and reach out to him. I treated him as if he were answering my text. I looked up one day and he began to reply to my text. There was a time he was upset and wouldn't eat what I cooked. The food would sit there until I put it away. I continued to serve his meals everyday, then one day he ate.—Tijuana Killian

If God did it for others, then you are next! Are you willing to fast and pray for your spouse? Every day, I will share my experiences for each topic and then we will pray. You will breakthrough in your marriage. God is faithful and not slack concerning His promises. Take this 30 day challenge because giving up is not an option. Nothing is impossible with God and nothing is too hard for Him.

DAY ONE

Kindness

WHEN WE ARE KIND to our spouses, we are generous and friendly. It's easy to be rude in return when our spouses aren't kind to us. However, if we are in right standing with God, we are held accountable unto the Lord to do the right things. God is love and we must demonstrate it. We can't control what our spouses do, but we can control what we do. I can recall a time where my husband did something that hurt my feelings. My flesh wanted to retaliate and go off on him. I knew that God wouldn't be pleased, so I went into prayer for strength. I heard the Holy Spirit say, "Cook breakfast in the morning and go to bed. Don't worry about anything." I didn't want to go to sleep because I was worried. I truly had to trust God to fix it. The last thing that I wanted to do was prepare breakfast but God knows best. Well, in the morning, I obeyed the Lord and everything was better than okay. Kindness can go a long way. When someone is rude to you, love the devil out of them because love conquers all. The Holy Spirit will convict them or the person may feel bad for how they treated you. Remember, do your part, believe God, and He will do what He has promised.

I declare that my spouse will be kind, tenderhearted, and forgiving just as God in Christ forgave me (Ephesians 4:32).

I declare that my spouse will be kind and patient towards me in Jesus' name.

I declare that my spouse will never take out their frustrations on me in Jesus' name.

I decree Proverbs 11:17 over my spouse that they will be kind so they can benefit themself.

I decree Colossians 3:12 over my spouse that they are God's chosen ones, holy and beloved, compassionate, kind, humble, meek, and patient.

I decree Proverbs 31:26 that when my spouse opens their mouths, there is much wisdom and teaching of kindness upon their tongues.

I bind up any arrogance or rudeness from my spouse in Jesus' name.

I bind up any agitation and resentfulness off my spouse in the name of Jesus.

I decree that my spouse will not rejoice at wrongdoing but will rejoice with truth in Jesus' name.

Kindness

I decree that the love that my spouse has for me will love, believe, hope, and endure all things.

I decree that my spouse is kind to the poor and to those who are overlooked in society.

I decree that my spouse is kind and when an opportunity arises, they will do good to everyone, especially those in the household of faith (Galatians 6:10).

I decree that my spouse will not love in word or talk but in deed and in truth (1 John 3:18).

I decree that my spouse will not repay evil for evil but will be a blessing in Jesus' name (1 Peter 3:9).

I decree that my spouse has the fruits of the spirit operating strongly in their life. Lord, loose love, joy, peace, patience, kindness, goodness, faithfulness, gentleness, and temperance over them in Jesus' name.

Lord, bless my spouse to encourage me when I am down.

Lord, bless my spouse to be a comfort and show them how to love me in Jesus' name.

Lord, bless my spouse to be affectionate and have sympathy towards me.

Lord, bless my spouse and me to be on one accord and to have a sound mind.

I bind up rivalry, conceit, strife, and jealousy off my spouse in Jesus' name.

I bind up anger and domestic violence off my spouse in Jesus' name.

I decree that my spouse will count me more significant or esteem me higher than they do themselves.

I pray that my spouse won't be selfish by having a single's mentality in Jesus' name.

I decree that my spouse will not only look to their own interest but look to my interest as well.

I pray that my spouse will love me earnestly in Jesus' name.

I pray that my spouse will live by Acts 20:35 that it is more blessed to give than to receive.

I decree Colossians 3:14 that my spouse will put on love which binds everything together in perfect harmony.

I pray that my spouse and I will serve each other unto you Lord.

Kindness

I pray that my spouse will treat me how they want to be treated in Jesus' name.

I pray that my spouse will be kind to me even when it's not immediately reciprocated.

Lord, bless my spouse to speak life into my purpose and destiny in Jesus' name.

Lord, bless my spouse to speak kind words that will build me up in Jesus' name.

I pray that my spouse will show me unfailing kindness all the days of their life.

I decree that my spouse's kind words will be like honey to my soul and bring healing in Jesus' name (Proverbs 16:23-24).

I decree Proverbs 21:21 that my spouse will pursue righteousness and kindness so they can find life, righteousness, and honor.

I pray that my spouse will let go of any grudges and allow the Lord to heal them of any hidden pain in Jesus' name.

I bind up any revenge and fault finding in Jesus' name.

I bind up the spirit of hatred in Jesus' name.

I pray that my spouse will be a person after God's own heart.

I pray that my spouse will be merciful and extend the same grace that they desire when they stumble in Jesus' name.

Lord, bless my spouse to apply Your Word in every area of their lives in Jesus' name.

Lord, bless my spouse to pray for me as much as I pray for them.

Lord, bless my spouse to go above and beyond to extend kindness towards me.

DAY TWO

Loving

*L*OVING IS BEING AFFECTIONATE towards our spouses. We want the best for them and for them to prosper. My husband thanked me for loving him because he knows he can be difficult at times. God can place a love in our hearts for our spouses to love them the way they need. My husband and I have history. We have been through some things that most couples have never experienced. We can truly say that we are not in it for the money. Years ago, someone gave my husband a prophecy concerning me. They said, "Brother Tron, I had a dream that you were at a church preaching. You said that when you met your wife that you had nothing." When my husband told me about this prophecy, we both chuckled because we met when we were both at a low point in life. Love can hold the marriage together because it is patient and kind.

I decree that my spouse will love me as Christ loves the Church.

I decree that my spouse will show loving-kindness towards me in Jesus' name.

I decree that my spouse will go above and beyond to bestow love upon me.

Lord, show my spouse how to love me in the name of Jesus.

I declare that my spouse will do everything in love.

I decree that my spouse will love me in the good and bad times.

I decree that my spouse will love me through thick and thin in Jesus' name.

I decree that my spouse will defend me and esteem me highly in the name of Jesus.

I bind up jealousy and every evil work that will try to come against my spouse and I in Jesus' name.

I decree that my spouse radiates the love and presence of God.

Lord, I thank You that my spouse's love towards me covers a multitude of sins.

Lord, bless my spouse to love me in sickness and in health.

Lord, bless my spouse to love me in riches and poverty.

Lord, bless my spouse to have my back and cut off toxic relationships in Jesus' name.

Lord, bestow faithfulness and commitment upon my spouse.

I decree that my spouse desires me above anyone else in the name of Jesus.

Lord, keep my spouse from falling into temptation.

Lord, remove any seductress out of my spouse's path in Jesus' name.

I bind up any wandering eyes and decree that my spouse only has eyes for me in Jesus' name.

Lord, bless my spouse to do the right thing always in the name of Jesus.

Lord, bless my spouse to take care of me and be devoted to our marriage in the name of Jesus.

I bind up any secrets in our marriage in the name of Jesus.

I decree that my spouse will encourage and speak life into me in the name of Jesus.

Lord, bless my spouse to demonstrate Your love in their life in Jesus' name.

I decree Ephesians 4:2 that my spouse will be humble, gentle, patient, and loving towards me.

I decree that my spouse will love me deeply and will never break my heart in Jesus' name.

Lord, bless my marriage to be an example of a Kingdom marriage in the name of Jesus.

I decree Song of Solomon 4:9 that I will captivate my spouse's heart.

I bind up empty promises in the name of Jesus.

I decree that my spouse and I will flirt and date often in Jesus' name.

I bind up any abandonment and covenant-breaking spirits in Jesus' name.

I bind up any selfish and sabotaging spirits in Jesus' name.

Lord, bless my spouse to love You with their whole heart so they can love me properly in the name of Jesus.

I decree Romans 12:10 that my spouse will be devoted to me in love and honor me above themself.

Lord, bless my spouse and I to submit to one another out of reverence for You.

Loving

Lord, bless me to love my spouse the way You created them to be loved.

Lord, bless my spouse to love and treat me right so their prayers will not be hindered.

Lord, bless my spouse to love themself so they can love me.

Lord, bless my spouse to love me as they would love their own body.

Lord, give my spouse a revelation of who You are and allow them to get Your word in their hearts so they will not sin against You.

DAY THREE

No Selfishness

ONE OF THE BENEFITS of marriage is to share your life with someone. It's easy to think only of yourself. However in marriage, that will not work. Not being selfish involves us considering others. When I first met my husband, we had different tastes. I love ground turkey and he loves ground beef. He has been unwilling to try the leaner meat. At first, I would only cook meals with ground turkey because my mentality was, "If you don't eat what I cook, then starve." As a wife, I have to make sure my husband has a hot meal on the table. I now cook more food with both ground turkey and ground beef. Love isn't selfish, but it's serving.

I decree that my spouse will not be selfish in Jesus' name.

I decree Philippians 2:4 that my spouse is not only looking out for their own interest but mine as well.

I bind up the works of the flesh in my marriage in Jesus' name.

No Selfishness

I decree that my spouse will not be a lover of self, conceited, greedy, proud, or arrogant in Jesus' name.

I decree that my spouse will not be abusive, disobedient to their parents, or leadership in Jesus' name.

I decree that my spouse will not be ungrateful but will appreciate what they have at home in the name of Jesus.

I decree that my spouse will not be unholy or heartless in the name of Jesus.

I decree that my spouse will not be slanderous, treacherous, reckless, or caught up in foolishness in Jesus' name.

I decree that my spouse will not turn a blind eye to those who may have a need in the name of Jesus.

I decree that the love of God will abide in my spouse in the name of Jesus.

I pray that when my spouse makes decisions, they will consider our family in the name of Jesus.

I bind up the single mentality in my marriage in the name of Jesus.

I pray that my spouse will go above and beyond to please me and to make sure that I am satisfied in the name of Jesus.

I pray that my spouse will spend a lifetime making me happy in the name of Jesus.

I pray that my spouse will constantly make me smile in the name of Jesus.

I pray that my spouse will be a blessing when it's in their power to do so in the name of Jesus.

I bind up rivalry or conceit in my marriage in the name of Jesus.

I pray that my spouse counts me more significant than they do themself in the name of Jesus.

I bind up the spirit of manipulation and control in the name of Jesus.

I bind up witchcraft off my marriage in the name of Jesus.

I bind up narcissistic behavior off my spouse in the name of Jesus.

I bind up evil agendas off my spouse in the name of Jesus.

I declare that my spouse's motives will be pure in the name of Jesus.

I decree that my spouse will help me when needed in the name of Jesus.

No Selfishness

I decree that my spouse will be concerned with my health and wellness in the name of Jesus.

I bind up stinginess and mistreatment in the name of Jesus.

I bind up selfish motives and dysfunction in the name of Jesus.

I bind up strife and division in my home in the name of Jesus.

I decree that the enemy will not use my spouse against me in the name of Jesus.

I bind up the spirit of retaliation in the name of Jesus.

I pray that my spouse is compassionate and giving in the name of Jesus.

I pray that my spouse will work hard for the good of the family in the name of Jesus.

I bind up destruction and sabotage in the name of Jesus.

I pray that my spouse will allow the Lord to order and guide their steps.

I bind up unrighteousness, wrath, fury, and lust in the name of Jesus.

I pray that my spouse and I are partners and friends in the name of Jesus.

Lord bless my spouse and I to always work together as a team in the name of Jesus.

I pray that my spouse will be dead to self and alive unto God in Jesus' name.

DAY FOUR

Provider

IT'S GREAT TO BRING something to the table so all the burden won't be on one person. When my husband and I got married, we went through a wilderness experience. He lost his job and couldn't find work for years. All the financial burden was on me. At times, funds were tight and we couldn't do much but God always made a way for us. Our marriage made it through the dry season and when we got out, my husband received supernatural backpay. He got a great paying job with benefits and his business began to succeed. It's a blessing to have the burdens lifted and my husband providing for the family. I love it when my husband surprises me with gifts, flowers, chocolates, or takes me out. He appreciates that I stood with him when he was going through a tough time. He wants to make sure that he cherishes me. If you are going through something similar, God will provide and bring your family out.

I decree that my spouse is a great provider in the name of Jesus.

Lord, open up the heavens over my family so money will never be an issue.

Lord, supply all of my family's needs according to your riches and glory in Jesus' name. Amen.

The Lord is my Shepherd. My family shall not want.

Lord, if we delight ourselves in You, we will receive the desires of our hearts.

I bind up anxiousness in the name of Jesus.

Lord, bless my spouse and I with a supernatural promotion.

Lord, bring increase into my family.

Lord, enlarge my family's territory.

Lord, direct my spouse's and my path in the name of Jesus.

I bind up every hole in my family's pocket in the name of Jesus.

I command money to come forth from the north, south, east, and west in the name of Jesus.

Lord, prosper my family.

I pray that my spouse will work hard for our family.

Provider

I pray that my spouse will be diligent.

The hands of the diligent make them rich.

I bind up any lazy and slothful spirit in the name of Jesus.

I bind up procrastination and excuse making in the name of Jesus.

I bind up fear in the name of Jesus.

I decree that money will not change my spouse.

I decree that my spouse will love you Lord more than money.

I decree that my spouse will never sell out to greed in the name of Jesus.

I decree that my spouse is full of faith and reaps financial breakthroughs in the name of Jesus.

Lord, led my spouse and I into greener pastures in the name of Jesus.

Lord, You provide a thousand cattles on a hill.

Lord, lead my spouse and I to our promised Land.

Lord, lead my spouse and I to a land flowing with milk and honey.

Lord, lead my spouse and I into a land of Goshen.

Lord, favor my spouse with you and man.

Lord, anoint my spouse with oil and allow their cups to flow over.

Lord, bless my spouse with an overflow.

Lord, give my spouse wisdom on the way to provide for our family.

Lord, bless my spouse to build up your Kingdom and our household.

Lord, bless my spouse to be a good steward over what you have given them.

Lord, bless my spouse to have a great job with benefits in Jesus' name.

Lord, bless my spouse to have a great retirement package.

Lord, bless my spouse to always have money in the bank.

I bind up financial strain and tension on our marriage in Jesus' name.

Provider

I bind up lack off my family in Jesus' name.

I bind up generation curses in the name of Jesus.

I decree that my spouse and I are sufficient in all things at all times in Jesus name.

I pray that my spouse and I will abound in every good work.

I decree that the Lord is our helper.

I pray that our barns will be filled with plenty.

I pray that our vats will be bursting with wine.

Thank You, Lord, for always providing a ram in the bush.

I bind up any unemployment in the name of Jesus.

I pray that my spouse will always have a great cash flow in the name of Jesus.

I pray that my spouse and I are wealthy in the name of Jesus.

I bind up any financial attacks in the name of Jesus.

I decree that famine and economic crashes will never affect my family in the name of Jesus.

Lord, strengthen my spouse as they work hard for our family in Jesus' name.

I bind up any demonic attacks on my spouse's job in the name of Jesus.

I pray that my spouse will be protected at work from harm.

Lord, bless my spouse to be healthy so they can continue to work for our family in Jesus' name.

Lord, bless my spouse with peace and great focus as they are working to take care of our family in the name of Jesus.

DAY FIVE

Protector

PROTECTING IS GUARDING SOMEONE that you care about and that is what my husband has always done for me. He is 6'2 and I'm 5'2. His height and strength make me feel secure. Not only does my husband protect me physically but he defends my reputation. In ministry, some people hate me for no legit reason. When people say mean things about me in his inbox or social media, he takes up for me. I thank God that He sent me a husband, who has my back. One night I came home from work and a huge stray dog was on my porch. I am terrified of big dogs because I was attacked years ago by one when I went to visit a friend. Immediately, I called my husband on the phone and he came outside with no fear. He had a broom in his hand and shooed the dog off the porch. Then he walked to my car door, opened it, and escorted me into the house. I am grateful to have a spouse that makes me feel safe. He holds me at night and massages my scalp. God will bless you with a spouse who will protect you in every way.

Lord, bless my spouse to be bold.

Lord, bless my spouse to defend me publicly in Jesus' name.

Lord, bless my spouse to go out of their way to protect me from harm in the name of Jesus.

Lord, bless my spouse to be strong, so they can protect me from natural attacks,

Lord, bless my spouse to war in the spirit on my behalf.

Lord, bless my spouse with discernment so no one will ever take advantage of me.

Lord, bless my spouse to discern witches, warlocks, agents of Satan, and those with evil motives that want to connect to me in Jesus' name.

Lord, bless me to be humble to receive godly counsel from my spouse in the name of Jesus.

Lord, speak to my spouse regularly concerning my life, purpose, and destiny.

Lord, bless the wrong people to be removed from both myself and my spouse's life in the name of Jesus.

Lord, give my spouse strength to cut off toxic relationships in the name of Jesus.

Lord, bless my spouse with wisdom on how to lead and engage in conversation in the name of Jesus.

Lord, give my spouse a burden of prayer and fasting so they can go to another level in You.

Lord, bless my spouse to always guard me in the name of Jesus.

Lord, bless my spouse to never cheat on me in the name of Jesus.

Lord, bless my spouse to treat my heart with tenderness so they will never break it in the name of Jesus.

Lord, bless my spouse to keep boundaries when it comes to the opposite sex in the name of Jesus.

Lord, bless my spouse to treat me like royalty in the name of Jesus.

Lord, if my in-laws ever get out of hand, bless my spouse to stand up for me in the name of Jesus.

Lord, bless my spouse to protect my reputation in the name of Jesus.

Lord, bless my spouse to protect my feelings in the name of Jesus.

Lord, bless my spouse to protect me sexually. I decree they will never step out of our marriage and bring back diseases.

Lord, bless my spouse to respect who I am in the name of Jesus.

Lord, bless my spouse to speak life into me when I need encouragement in the name of Jesus.

Lord, bless my spouse to stand their ground to defend our marriage if anyone ever comes against us in the name of Jesus.

Lord, place a hedge of protection around my spouse and I.

Lord, cancel any demonic attacks concerning my spouse.

Lord, bless my spouse with a long life.

I bind up stress off my spouse in Jesus' name.

Lord, loose an anointing upon my spouse for peace and courage in the name of Jesus.

Lord, order my spouse's steps to be in the right place at the right time in the name of Jesus.

I bind up any tragedies concerning my spouse.

I rebuke scandals and evilness from being associated with my spouse.

I bind up any plagues from coming near my spouse in Jesus' name.

Lord, guard my spouse from the evil one in the name of Jesus.

Lord, send angels to guard my spouse and I in Jesus' name.

I bind up premature death in the name of Jesus.

I decree that no weapon formed against my spouse and I will prosper in the name of Jesus.

Lord, vindicate my spouse and I from any wrongdoing in the name of Jesus.

Lord, avenge us when our enemies come against us.

Lord, hide my spouse and I in the shadow of Your wings.

Lord, thank You for being with my spouse and I in the name of Jesus.

I decree that my spouse and I will not be dismayed but will use our authority in the name of Jesus Christ.

Lord, bless my spouse to put on Your full armor (armor of God) daily.

Lord, bless my spouse to set their face like a flint and never shrink back in the name of Jesus.

DAY SIX

Friend

A FRIEND IS SOMEONE SPECIAL that you have a bond with, enjoy conversing, can hold your secrets, love you despite the flaws, and has your back. Our spouses should be our best friends. We must like our spouses even when things get difficult. That's the beauty of going through the storm. You have someone to go through with you. My husband and I started off as friends. When we met, I was going to court almost every week with my children's father. It was a depressing time and I would cry often. My husband would text me and encourage me to hold on for God's best. I looked forward to his messages because they brighten my day. If there is a disconnect, God can unify the bond between you and your spouse.

I decree that my spouse and I are best friends in the name of Jesus.

I decree that we enjoy each other's company and get along great in the name of Jesus.

I decree that we will miss each other when we aren't around each other in Jesus' name.

I decree that my spouse and I will be attracted to one another in Jesus' name.

I decree that the passion is strong in my marriage.

Lord, bless my spouse and I to bond and build memories in Jesus' name.

Lord, bless my spouse and I to cover one another's flaws.

Lord, bless my spouse and I to love one another through the trials in life.

Lord, bless my spouse and I never to hit below the belt by using hurtful things against one another.

Lord, bless my spouse and I to have awesome communication.

I bind up division, strife, and miscommunication in Jesus' name.

Lord, bless my spouse and I to trust one another in a deeper way.

Lord, bless my spouse and I to date regularly.

Lord, bless my spouse and I to invest in our marriage.

Lord, bless my spouse and I never to neglect one another in Jesus' name.

I bind up distance in the name of Jesus.

I bind up jealousy and insecurity in the name of Jesus.

Lord, bless my spouse and I to have each other's backs in Jesus' name.

Lord, bless my spouse and I to treat each other right so You can get the glory.

I decree Proverbs 17:17 over my spouse and I that a friend will love at all times.

Lord, remove anyone out of my spouse's path that is sent to destroy our marriage in Jesus' name.

Lord, bless my spouse and I to sharpen one another in Jesus' name.

Lord, You put my spouse and I together for a purpose. Bless us to always be mindful of this fact.

I decree Ecclesiastes 4:9 that two are better than one because we have a good reward for our labor.

Lord, I thank You that if my spouse and I fall, we can lift each other up.

Lord, thank You for the companionship in my marriage.

Lord, bless my spouse and I never to take for granted that we keep each other warm at night.

I bind up arguments and drama in my marriage in Jesus' name.

I decree that a threefold cord is not easily broken in Jesus' name (Ecclesiastes 4:12).

I decree 1 Thessalonians 5:11 that my spouse and I will encourage and build one another up.

I decree Proverbs 27:9 that the sweetness of a friend comes with earnest counsel.

I decree that my spouse and I will not attack each other like we are enemies.

Lord, bless my spouse and I to be humble so we can receive counsel from each other.

I bind up unforgiveness, fault finding, offenses, and grumbling in Jesus' name.

Friend

Lord, bless my spouse and I to treat each other like Kings and Queens.

Lord, bless my spouse and I to appreciate each other as gifts.

Lord, bless my spouse and I to be in right alignment with You so order can be established in our home.

Lord, bless my spouse to treat me the way they wanted to be treated.

Lord, bless my spouse to strengthen my faith and motivate me to go deeper into You.

Lord, bless my spouse and I to demonstrate Your love for each other in Jesus' name.

I bind up betrayal and hurt in my marriage in Jesus' name.

DAY SEVEN

Priority

WHEN SOMEONE IS A priority, you make them number one or at the top of your list. God needs to be first place then our spouses next. It's out of order when we put our children before our spouses. When God is first, then everything else will line up. When things are out of God's order then it's chaotic. My husband doesn't put his family before me. He constantly considers my feelings and does things to make sure that I know how special I am to him. Even though we both are busy with work, we make time for date nights. Monday through Friday, I do ministry and the weekends are family time. We have to invest in our marriage because it does us no good when we are saving the world and our homes are a mess. Things are peaceful and smooth when you come home after a long day to an atmosphere of love.

Lord, bless my spouse to make me a priority underneath You.

Lord, let order be established in my home.

Priority

I decree first it's the Lord, then the husband, wife, and kids in the name of Jesus.

Lord, bless my spouse never to put the children, siblings, or in-laws in front of me in the name of Jesus.

Lord, bless my spouse and I to overcome any challenge in the name of Jesus.

Lord, bless my spouse and I to have balance in our marriage.

Lord, bless my spouse and I never to neglect each other in Jesus' name.

I pray that my spouse and I will give each other the attention that we desire.

Lord, bless my spouse and I to make time for one another.

Lord, bless my spouse and I to invest in our marriage in Jesus' name.

Lord, bless my spouse to be open to counsel if we need it.

I bind up pride and rebellion out of my marriage in Jesus' name.

I bind up control and manipulation in the name of Jesus.

I bind up witchcraft coming against my marriage in Jesus' name.

Lord, bless my spouse to treat me with the utmost respect in the name of Jesus.

I pray that my spouse will always make me feel special and significant in Jesus' name.

Lord, bless my spouse to take interest in some things that are important to me in Jesus' name.

Lord, bless my spouse and I to focus on what's important in the name of Jesus.

Lord, bless my spouse and I to find ways to connect and bond more in Jesus' name.

Lord, bless my spouse and I to satisfy each other's needs.

I bind up infidelity and wandering eyes in the name of Jesus.

I bind up divorce and covenant-breaking spirits in the name of Jesus.

Lord, bless my spouse to be in right alignment with You so everything else in our home can fall into place.

Lord, bless my spouse to fall deeper in love with You so they can love me the way Your word commands.

Priority

Lord, bless my spouse to love You with their whole heart, souls, and strength.

Lord, bless my spouse to yield to Your conviction when they get out of order.

Lord, bless my spouse and I to submit to one another unto You.

Lord, bless my spouse to serve one another in love.

Lord, bless my spouse and I to be affectionate towards each other.

I bind up selfishness out of my marriage.

I bind up loneliness in the name of Jesus.

I bind up division in the name of Jesus.

Lord, bless my spouse and I to live in harmony with one another.

Lord, bless my spouse and I to keep people out of our marriage in Jesus' name.

Lord, bless my spouse and I to work together as a team.

Lord, bless my spouse and I to make decisions together.

Lord, bless my spouse and I to compromise with each other.

Lord, bless my spouse and I to be understanding of each other's needs.

I bind up reckless behavior in the name of Jesus.

Lord, bless my spouse to always have my back in the name of Jesus.

Lord, heal the broken areas of my marriage in Jesus' name.

Lord, bless my spouse and I to seek Your Kingdom and righteousness first so everything else can be added unto us.

Lord, bless my spouse and I to listen to each other's dreams and aspirations in Jesus' name.

Lord, bless my spouse and I to build and work towards our goals in Jesus' name.

I bind up idolatry in our marriage.

I pray that my spouse and I will not idolize each other.

Lord, I pray that my spouse and I will not be distracted when we spend time together.

Priority

I decree that my spouse and I will not reschedule our dates or plans to put other people first.

I pray that my spouse and I will always be honest with one another in Jesus' name.

Lord, order my spouse and my steps in the name of Jesus.

DAY EIGHT

Understanding

When we have an understanding about something, we comprehend it. God specializes in divine connections. He surrounds us with those who can support and celebrate the vision that He gave us. God put us with our spouses as partners on a team. My husband and I have a vlog called, "Team Moses." My husband always desired to vlog when we got married and when he met me, that's what we did. I'm sometimes amazed at how my husband and I can understand each other's needs. We must keep this fact at the back of our minds because the enemy creeps into relationships and makes couples feel disconnected. At vulnerable times, the devil will try to cause a false connection with someone who isn't our spouse. Many affairs resulted because someone felt like their spouse didn't understand them anymore. God can keep the love strong in our marriages and restore the broken bond.

I pray that my spouse will be understanding of my needs in Jesus' name.

Understanding

Lord, bless my spouse to be aware of my feelings and be forgiving in the name of Jesus.

Lord, bless my spouse to have prophetic insight into my destiny so they can pray for me effectively.

Lord, bless my spouse to understand my spiritual call in the name of Jesus.

Lord, give my spouse and I wisdom to have a successful marriage in Jesus' name.

Lord, bless my spouse and I to work on ourselves so we can become better spouses.

I bind up instability in my marriage in Jesus' name.

I bind up selfishness in the name of Jesus.

I bind up division and strife in the name of Jesus.

Lord, bless my spouse and I to be totally committed to one another.

I pray that my spouse and I will never take each other for granted.

I pray that my spouse and I will appreciate each other.

I pray that my spouse and I will fight for our marriage by working hard to make it work.

I pray that my spouse and I will stay in God's will.

I decree that my spouse and I are happily married.

Lord bless my spouse and I to work through misunderstandings.

Lord, bless my spouse and I to have healthy conflict resolution.

Lord, bless my spouse and I to have discernment, so we don't get caught up in demonic pitfalls.

Lord, bless my spouse and I to have realistic expectations in our marriage.

Lord, bless my spouse and I to learn from our mistakes and not repeat them in Jesus' name.

Lord, establish the bond of trust between my spouse and I in a deeper way.

Lord, bless my spouse and I to support each other through thick and thin.

Lord, strengthen the intimacy between my spouse and I.

Understanding

Lord, let compassion, unity, friendship, and partnership increase in our marriage.

Lord, bless my spouse and I to understand our differences.

Lord, bless my spouse and I to appreciate each other's uniqueness.

Lord, show my spouse and I how to love each other.

Lord, I pray that my spouse and I are never judgmental of each other.

Lord, I pray that my spouse and I never feel like we have lost ourselves in our marriage.

Lord, show my spouse what's important to me.

Lord, bless my spouse to be humble and esteem me better than they do themselves.

Lord, bless my spouse to work hard for our family.

I pray against foolish behavior in my marriage.

I bind up wrath and hastiness in the name of Jesus.

Lord, soften my spouse's heart towards You and Your word.

Lord, bless my spouse and I with a greater understanding of who You are so we can keep your law and observe it with our whole heart (Psalm 119:34).

Lord, bless my spouse and I to be patient with one another.

Lord, bless my spouse and I to be a great support system to each other.

I bind up resentment in the name of Jesus.

Lord, bless my spouse and I to have the utmost respect and admiration for each other.

Lord, bless my spouse not to fault find or keep records of wrong doings.

I bind up rejection in the name of Jesus.

I bind disappointment in the name of Jesus.

Lord, bless my spouse and I to build each other.

I bind up stony hearts in the name of Jesus.

Lord, bless my spouse and I to have a Kingdom marriage.

DAY NINE

Great Listener

A GREAT LISTENER IS PATIENT and makes you feel like what you are saying is of the utmost importance. When you and your spouse were courting, you guys probably talked on the phone for hours and couldn't get enough of each other. When people are courting, they are on their best behavior and being a great listener is what they do because they want to know everything about each other. However, when time goes on, some people may lose interest and tune out their spouse. That's not good. Our spouse is a part of us and what they care about, we should too. Listening is a part of having great communication. We have to communicate to have a great marriage. My husband listens to me, telling the same stories. He knows that I love to talk and go down memory lane. Yet, he listens like it's brand new information. God can strengthen the communication skills in your marriage.

I decree that my spouse is a great listener in Jesus' name.

I decree James 1:19 that my spouse will be quick to hear, slow to speak, and slow to anger.

I decree Proverbs 19:20 that my spouse will listen to advice and accept instruction, that they may gain wisdom in the future.

I pray that my spouse won't give an answer before they hear something because that's folly and will lead to shame.

I pray Proverbs 2:2 that my spouse will have an attentive ear to wisdom and incline their heart to understanding.

I pray that my spouse has an ear to hear so they can hear.

Lord, I pray that my spouse will never stray from Your words of knowledge.

Lord, I pray that my spouse will listen to You so they can dwell secure and be at ease.

Lord, bless my spouse to be humble so they will take heed to correction lest they fall.

Lord, bless my spouse to be in sync with Your spirit so they can always hear Your voice.

Lord, bless my spouse to obey Your instructions so our household can be blessed.

Lord, bless my spouse to be full of faith and Your word.

Lord, bless my spouse to listen when I express my feelings.

Great Listener

Lord, bless my spouse and I to have great communication.

Lord, bless my spouse and I not to yell at each other when having a conversation.

Lord, bless my spouse and I not to cut each other off when we are talking.

Lord, I pray that my spouse never has a deaf ear and tune me out in Jesus' name.

Lord, bless my spouse to have the right body language when we are communicating.

I bind up any miscommunication and division in Jesus' name.

I bind up strife and arguments in the name of Jesus.

Lord, bless my spouse and I not to be distracted when we are having a conversation.

Lord, bless my spouse not to judge me when they hear something they don't like.

Lord, bless my spouse with wisdom so we can communicate effectively.

I pray that my spouse is not only a hearer of the word but a doer.

Lord, I pray that my spouse's heart is in the right posture with You so they can receive the deeper things of the spirit.

Proverbs 12:15 says that the way of a fool is right in his own eyes, but a wise man listens to advice.

Proverbs 10:17 says that whoever heeds instruction is on the path to life but he who rejects reproof leads others astray.

I decree Proverbs 1:5 that the wise hear and increase in learning, and the one who understands obtain guidance.

I decree 1 Peter 3:12 over my spouse for the eyes of the Lord are on the righteous and his ears are open to their prayer.

I decree Luke 11:28 over my spouse that they are blessed because they hear the word of God and keep it.

I decree that my spouse is the Lord's sheep and His sheep knows His voice.

Lord, bless my spouse to hear Your voice in the midst of the storm.

Lord, bless my spouse to love You with their whole heart so they won't sin against You.

Lord, bless my spouse to consider my needs in the name of Jesus.

Great Listener

Lord, bless my spouse to take heed to godly counsel lest they stumble.

In the multitude of counsel, there is safety.

Lord, bless my spouse to discern Your voice from the voice of the enemy.

I pray that my spouse will be attentive to my needs in Jesus' name.

I pray that my spouse will listen to me with empathy.

I pray that my spouse will listen to me lovingly and generously.

I pray that my spouse will listen without bias.

I pray that my spouse will always make time for me and listen to my opinion.

I pray that my spouse will make eye contact and hold my hand in the name of Jesus.

DAY TEN

Great Communication

Some people can't communicate without arguing. Others don't even speak to each other. Some people are easily offended and hold back their words. It's not God's will for us to be at our spouse's throats or tear each other down with our words. When we hurt our spouses, we are hurting ourselves. We have to remember that our spouse is not our enemy. God put them in our lives to help us and to pray for us. Most men don't like people telling them what to do. They are leaders and desire respect. However, they must trust the godly counsel from their spouse. I am my husband's prophet, whether he likes it or not. The truth hurts and I tell him that even if it gets on his nerves. One day, my husband was really sick. He stayed in bed for a week and I begged him to go to the doctor. Men can be stubborn, but I wasn't taking no for an answer. I told him that I was too young to be a widow and we are going to the hospital. Well, he listened and the doctor told him that he had COVID. After we left, my husband repented and he listens better now. He knows I have his best

Great Communication

interest. We must humble ourselves because in the multitude of counselors, there is safety.

I decree that my spouse and I have great communication in Jesus' name.

I bind up strife in Jesus' name.

I bind up division in the name of Jesus.

I bind up drama in the name of Jesus.

I bind up demonic attacks in the name of Jesus.

I bind up miscommunication in the name of Jesus.

Lord, loose peace in my home in the name of Jesus.

Lord, loose unity in the name of Jesus.

Lord, loose love in the name of Jesus.

I bind up pride in my spouse in the name of Jesus.

I decree that my spouse and I can communicate effectively in the name of Jesus.

I decree that my spouse and I will not disrespect each other.

I bind up divorce and separation in Jesus' name.

I bind up any demonic influence or suggestions in the name of Jesus.

Lord, silence the voice of the accuser of the brethren in Jesus' name.

Lord, bless my spouse and I to resolve conflict according to Matthew 18.

Lord, loose Your truth in my home in Jesus' name.

Lord, let Your presence be strong in my home in Jesus' name.

I bind up bitterness and unforgiveness in Jesus' name.

I pray that my spouse and I will not allow the sun to go down on our wrath.

Lord, bless my spouse and I to resolve issues and not run from them.

Lord, keep watch over our mouths.

Lord, bless my spouse and I to not hold grudges in Jesus' name.

Lord, bless my spouse and I not to say things that will grieve Your Spirit.

Great Communication

Lord, I repent for saying things that hurt my spouse in Jesus' name.

Lord, allow me to listen to what my spouse has to say.

Lord, bless my spouse and I to be patient with one another.

Lord, bless my spouse and I to have loving communication.

Lord, bless my spouse not to get offended when I say something.

Lord, bless my spouse to take heed to the counsel that You gave me for them.

I pray that my spouse and I will speak words of edification to one another.

I pray that my spouse and I will affirm one another.

I pray that my spouse and I will speak life into each other's purpose.

I pray that my spouse and I won't speak death or negative words over each other when we get upset.

I pray that my spouse and I will be quick to hear, slow to speak, and slow to anger.

I decree Ephesians 4:29 that no corrupt communication will come out of our mouths.

I decree Proverbs 15:1 that a soft answer turns away wrath. I will not speak harshly because it will only stir up anger.

I decree Psalm 141:3 that the Lord will set a guard over our mouths and keep watch over the door of our lips.

I decree Colossians 4:6 that our speech will be gracious and seasoned with salt.

Lord, let my spouse and I bring healing to each other with our words.

Lord, bless my spouse and I refrain from hurting one another.

Lord, give my spouse and I wisdom on how to communicate with each other.

I decree Colossians 3:8 that my spouse and I will put away anger, wrath, malice, slander, and obscene talk.

Lord, bless my spouse and I to speak truth in love.

I pray that my spouse and I will never give full vent to our spirits.

Lord, bless my spouse and I to renew our minds in Your Word.

Lord, bless my spouse and I apply Your Word to our marriage.

DAY ELEVEN

Patience

WHEN WE ARE PATIENT with our spouses, we aren't huffing and puffing. Our body language is calm and we aren't flustered. We don't rush our spouse to get to the point. We wait for them to express their thoughts. God uses our spouse to work patience in us. When my husband waits for me to go to the store, he learned patience over time. Sometimes I have to put on my makeup, do my hair, and put on something cute. Sometimes, I dress down. We can joke about this now. At first, my husband used to text me, "Hurry up." Now he just waits until I get ready. Love is patient and we just have to appreciate our spouse while they are here. No one lives forever. My husband told me, "I waited thirteen years for you, so I can wait just a while longer as you get ready. Babe, take as much time as you need. I love and cherish you. People are losing their spouses daily in this COVID-19 pandemic. I'm glad that we have each other."

I decree that my spouse will be patient with me.

I decree that my spouse won't be frustrated with me when I'm trying to communicate.

Patience

I pray that my spouse won't have the wrong body language when we are communicating.

I pray that my spouse won't cut me off or dismiss my opinions.

I pray that my spouse and I will be patient as we wait for the promises of God.

Lord, bless my spouse to get to know me more.

Lord, bless my spouse and I to rejoice and count it all joy when we go through all kinds of tribulation.

Lord, bless my spouse and I to do Your will so we can receive what's promised.

Lord, bless my spouse to be patient and partner with me as we face challenging situations.

Lord, bless my spouse to produce the fruits of the spirit: love, joy, peace, patience, kindness, goodness, faithfulness, and self-control.

I pray that my spouse will hear the word of God, hold it fast in an honest and good heart, and bear fruit with patience.

Lord, bless my spouse to accept my flaws and love me through them.

Lord strengthen my spouse with your power according to Your glorious might with all endurance and patience with joy.

I pray that my spouse will wait patiently on the Lord when making major decisions.

Thank You, Lord, for blessing my spouse and I with some awesome communication.

Lord, bless my spouse not to grow weary of doing good because they will reap if they faint not.

Lord, continue to produce endurance, faith, and godly character in my spouse.

Lord, bless my spouse to have a patient spirit with others.

Lord, bless my spouse and I to always dedicate quiet time together.

I bind up anxiety off of my spouse in Jesus' name.

I pray that my spouse will not allow things to stress them out.

I decree Romans 12:12 over my spouse that they will rejoice in hope, be patient in tribulation, and constant in prayer.

Patience

I pray Romans 8:25 over my spouse that they will hope for what they don't see and wait for it with patience.

I pray that my spouse will not fret over the wicked or the ones who prosper.

Lord, bless my spouse not to be impatient when it comes to making financial decisions.

God, you are not slow to fulfill Your promise in my spouse's life.

God, You are patient towards my spouse and I.

Lord, bless my spouse and I to allow each other to be ourselves.

Lord, I pray James 1:4 over my spouse that patience will have its perfect work so they can be complete, lacking in nothing.

Lord, bless my spouse not to give up when their faith is tested.

Lord, bless my spouse and I to trust each other.

Lord, bless my spouse to be sober-minded, dignified, self-controlled, sound in faith, loving, and full of Your word.

Lord, bless my spouse to help bear some pain or trials with me without complaining.

Lord, bless my spouse to be ready in season and out of season.

Lord bless my spouse and prosper their hands.

I decree Colossians 3:12 over my spouse that they are God's chosen, holy, beloved, compassionate, kind, humble, meek, and patient.

Lord, bless my spouse to be slow to anger.

Lord, bless my spouse not to be hasty with me.

Lord, bless my spouse to have rule over their spirit.

I decree Psalm 27:14 over my spouse that my spouse will wait on the Lord, be strong, and let their heart take courage.

Lord, bless my spouse to remain steadfast despite opposition, difficulty, or adversity.

Lord, bless my spouse to stick with me when things get tough and not blame me for things out of my control.

Lord, bless my spouse to be nurturing and tender-hearted towards me.

Lord, bless my spouse and I to fight for our marriage no matter the cost.

Patience

Lord, bless my spouse and I not to jump to conclusions or make assumptions.

Lord, bless my spouse to be respectful and forgiving towards me.

Lord, bless my spouse to be thoughtful and admire me.

DAY TWELVE

Forgiving

FORGIVING IS LETTING THINGS go without throwing it back up again in our spouse's faces. People will make mistakes and get us upset at times. However, if we have a relationship with Jesus, then we must forgive so He can forgive us of our sins. If we hold grudges, bitterness, hurt, sickness, demonic strongholds can set in. Marriage is symbolic of God's relationship with the church. The church is Christ's bride. God commands that a husband loves his wife as Christ loves the church. When we really love someone, we can overlook an offense. When my husband and I were courting, we got into a heated disagreement and broke up. We didn't speak for almost two months. We quickly realized that we loved each other and what we were fighting over truly didn't matter. Shortly after, we decided to give our relationships another shot and got engaged a few months later. We now laugh and joke about why we broke up. When you truly forgive someone, you can laugh with them and move forward in life. Whatever you are mad with your spouse about, let it go so God can bless your marriage.

Forgiving

I prophesy that your spouse will be forgiving and fight for your marriage no matter what.

Lord bless my spouse to forgive as You do.

Lord bless my spouse to let go of any offense and not keep records of wrong doings.

Lord heal my spouse of any hurt they may have hidden in their hearts.

I bind up the spirit of assault in Jesus' name.

Lord, bless my spouse never to throw my past in my face or use it against me.

Lord, bless my spouse to love me because love covers a multitude of sins.

Lord, allow my spouse to work through any challenges with me.

Lord, never allow my spouse to let anything get between us.

Lord, bless my spouse to cast all their cares upon you.

I bind up any sickness that will try to attach itself to my spouse due to unforgiveness.

I bind up any old hurts that will try to resurface in my spouse's soul.

I bind up any disappointments that will try to cling onto my spouse.

I bind up any petty annoyances that will try to get my spouse to turn against me in Jesus' name.

I bind up the spirit of betrayal in Jesus' name.

I bind up any insecurities that will manifest in my spouse.

I bind up the spirit of anger that will cause my spouse to view me as their enemy.

I bind up hatred and resentment that will try to penetrate my marriage in Jesus' name.

I decree that my spouse won't bury their hurt but yield it unto God for their deliverance.

I come against any emotional and mental trauma on my spouse in Jesus' name.

I decree that my spouse will never allow the enemy in their heart due to holding on to unforgiveness.

I bind up stress, pain, anxiety, jealousy, and sickness that will try to attach to my spouse due to unforgiveness.

Forgiving

I decree that my spouse will always be open and receptive to forgive me and others when we mess up.

I decree that my spouse will obey the Word of God with their whole heart.

I pray that my spouse will cast down every thought and high imagination that exalts itself against God.

I pray my spouse will never hurt me when they are hurting in Jesus' name.

I pray that my spouse will never take their anger out of me in the name of Jesus.

I pray that my spouse will never seek revenge or retribution when they get upset with me.

I bind up the spirit of retaliation in my marriage in Jesus' name.

Lord, if any trust has been broken in my marriage, please restore it.

Lord, fix the fragmented pieces of my marriage.

Lord, allow my marriage to be a Kingdom example in Your body.

I bind up any distance the enemy is trying to cause between my spouse and I.

I bind up any sexual problems or withholding due benevolence caused by unforgiveness.

I bind up any secrets and demonic influence out of my marriage in Jesus' name.

I decree Ephesians 4:32 over my spouse that they will be kind, tenderhearted, and forgiving towards me.

I bind up the enemy from trying to make my spouse and I to re-live painful moments in Jesus' name.

I bind up any judgmental spirit that would try to come on my spouse in Jesus' name.

Lord, bless my spouse and I to work through any problems and find a healthy way to resolve them.

I bind up any punishment or mistreatment in my marriage in Jesus' name.

I bind up any unforgiveness in Jesus' name.

Lord, if I turned anyone against my spouse, especially family when I vented, please forgive me and allow them to forgive my spouse as well.

Forgiving

Lord, bless my spouse and I never to bring yesterday's problems into today.

Lord, bless my spouse and I not to go to bed on any wrath.

Lord, bless my spouse and I not to act like strangers living in the same house.

Lord, bless my spouse and I not to run away from any problems but solve them through You.

Lord, thank You for giving my spouse and I the ministry of reconciliation.

DAY THIRTEEN

Encourager

*E*NCOURAGING SOMEONE INVOLVES US speaking words that are positive and uplifting. One of our jobs is to encourage our spouses when they go through trials. In ministry, people come and go. It hurts when the people you care about and helped in the past just cut you off. My husband sees how it hurts me and is always there to encourage me. He knows exactly what to say. It's a blessing to have someone speak life into you. I go through enough warfare outside of the home, so it's refreshing to have a husband encourage me. I also encourage him. A year into our marriage, he lost his passion for photography. He was turning down photoshoots left and right even when people begged him. He just didn't want to do it anymore. I pulled out almost every photo that I could find and encouraged him. I told him that he was one of the most anointed photographers that I have seen. God used that encouragement and shortly after, he started shooting again. Now his business is booming. Your spouse needs you to speak life into their destiny and assignment. When your spouse wins, so do you.

Lord, bless my spouse to be a great encourager to my life.

Lord, put your words of comfort in my spouse's mouth.

Lord, bless my spouse with wisdom and godly counsel in Jesus' name.

Lord, bless my spouse to impart the same comfort to me that they have received from You.

Lord, use my spouse mightily in the prophetic.

Lord, bless my spouse to speak life into my purpose, destiny, and ministry.

Lord, bless my spouse to be an inspiration to me and others.

Lord, bless my spouse to be a person of Your Word.

Lord, bless my spouse to motivate me when I want to give up.

Lord, bless my spouse to hold me accountable so I can always stay on track.

Lord, give my spouse discernment so they will have a heads up on the enemy.

Lord, show my spouse how to pray for me.

Lord, bless my spouse to help me in what I am called to do.

Lord, bless my spouse to be in my Amen corner in Jesus' name.

Lord, bless my spouse to be like a breath of fresh air to me and others.

Lord, bless my spouse to be positive and full of faith.

Lord, bless my spouse to be optimistic and hopeful in Your word.

Lord, let my spouse be a blessing to everyone they cross paths with.

Lord, bless my spouse to count it all joy when they go through various trials and tribulations.

Lord, bless my spouse to lean on Your strength and not their own.

Lord, encourage my spouse when they feel discouraged.

Lord, bless me with the right words to encourage my spouse.

Lord, bless my spouse and I to speak positive affirmations over each other.

Lord, bless my spouse to be proud of the work that I am doing for You.

Lord, bless my spouse to trust me with their darkest secrets or their feelings.

Lord, I pray that my spouse and I won't criticize each other's mistakes.

Lord, bless my spouse and I to appreciate each other's qualities.

I bind up ungratefulness from my marriage in Jesus' name.

I bind up the mindset that the grass is greener on the other side.

Lord, bless my spouse to always pray for me.

Lord, bless my spouse and I to bring out the best in each other.

Lord, bless my spouse to be there for me when I need them the most.

Lord, bless my spouse and I to stand by each other no matter what.

I bind up any covenant-breaking spirits in the name of Jesus.

I bind up division and competition in the name of Jesus.

Lord, bless my spouse to stay focused on Jesus Christ.

Lord, bless my spouse and I to hold our peace or be silent when it's necessary.

Lord, bless my spouse and I to speak each other's love languages.

Lord, bless my spouse to love, hug, touch, kiss, and hold hands often.

Lord, bless my spouse and I to date and enjoy each other's companionship.

Lord, bless my spouse and I to brag on each other in public.

Lord, bless my spouse and I to support and honor each other in front of our children or family.

Lord, I pray that my spouse and I will never overwhelm each other.

Lord, I pray that my spouse and I will take an interest in what we are both passionate about.

Lord, bless my spouse and I attraction to each other to be strong.

Lord, I pray that my spouse and I will never be harsh with one another.

Encourager

Lord, I pray that my spouse and I will never make each other feel stupid or incompetent.

Lord, bless my spouse and I to have with each other and build new memories.

Lord, bless my spouse and I to always have each other's back and defend one another.

Lord, bless my spouse and I to respect one another.

DAY FOURTEEN

Supporter

SUPPORTING SOMEONE IS BEING there for them, investing in them, and cheering them on. We need to be our spouse's biggest cheerleaders. I went through a season in my ministry where I felt invisible. It seemed like no one cared about what I was doing. I was happy when my husband was right by my side, supporting what I was called to do. I used to cry many nights because my books weren't selling and no one wanted to watch my preaching videos. My husband was on every call and promoted my ministry. When he stepped out in his assignment, I was there too. God wants us to support our spouses so they can be more effective in their God-given purpose. My husband lets me preach and it's a blessing because many people don't have support from their spouses. It doesn't matter who comes and goes. We have God and our spouses. We aren't alone. God is with us.

I pray that my spouse and I will always support one another.

Thank You, Lord, that I have a great support system at home in Jesus' name.

Supporter

I bind up loneliness in the name of Jesus.

I bind up the spirit of abandonment in the name of Jesus.

Lord, bless my spouse and I to be each other's biggest supporter.

Lord, bless my spouse and I to make each other a top priority in each other's lives.

Lord, bless my spouse and I to stand by each other no matter what.

Lord, bless my spouse and I to stand on Your promises.

Lord, strengthen my spouse's faith.

Lord, bless my spouse and I to allow each other to go forth in what we are called to do.

I bind up any jealousy or insecurity in the name of Jesus.

Lord, bless my spouse to take time off work or their schedule if needed to be with me during times of recognition or celebration.

Lord, give my spouse balance so they will never neglect their family.

Lord, bless my spouse to help me when I feel like the burden it's too heavy to carry by myself.

Lord, bless my spouse and I to have a listening ear when we are telling each other what's on our minds.

Lord, bless my spouse and I to be a team.

Lord, bless my spouse and I to always get along.

Lord, remove any discord out of our marriage in Jesus' name.

Lord, strengthen the bond between my spouse and I.

Lord, bless my spouse and I to promote one another's books, business, ministry, products, or services.

Lord, bless my spouse and I to always speak highly of one another.

Lord, bless my spouse and I to believe in each other's God-given vision.

Lord, bless my spouse and I to be willing to sacrifice for each other.

Lord, bless my spouse and I to war on each other's behalf.

Lord, bless my spouse and I to be proud of each other's accomplishments.

Lord, bless my spouse and I to inspire each other.

Lord, bless my spouse and I to treat each other with the utmost respect.

Lord, bless my spouse and I to spoil one another.

Lord, bless my spouse and I to invest in our marriage.

Lord, bless my spouse and I to always honor our commitment to each other.

Lord, bless my spouse and I to step up for each other when we are down or weak.

Lord, bless my spouse and I to always build each other up.

Lord, bless my spouse and I to submit to one another as unto You.

Lord, bless my spouse and I to live in perfect harmony.

Lord, bless my spouse and I to work well together.

Lord, show my spouse and I how to love and support one another.

Lord, bless my marriage to be healthy in Jesus' name.

I bind up any dysfunction in my marriage in Jesus' name.

Lord, bless my spouse and I to appreciate each other despite our shortcomings.

Lord, bless my spouse and I to grow spiritually in You.

Lord, bless my spouse and I to keep other people out of our marriage.

I bind up any negativity that will try to penetrate my marriage in Jesus' name.

Lord, bless my spouse and I to show our support to each other not only in word but in action.

Lord, bless my spouse and I to push each other to go higher.

Lord, bless my spouse and I to give each other godly counsel.

Lord, bless my spouse and I to give each other space or time to spend with You.

Lord, give my spouse and I wisdom on how to become mates.

Lord, strengthen our communication.

DAY FIFTEEN

Companion

A COMPANION IS KEEPING SOMEONE company. God never intended for a man to be alone. He gave Adam a help meet, Eve, to be his wife. God knows that there is strength in numbers. Loneliness can be depressing. However, people are strengthened with joy and happiness when they are surrounded by loved ones. I cried for three years because I desired marriage. I was so glad when God blessed me with a companion. God turned my mourning into dancing. Now, I enjoy traveling, cooking, and leisure time with my husband. He enjoys spending time with me as well. When he is at work, he texts and calls me when on his breaks because he misses me. God wants us to appreciate our spouses because they are a gift. Find out ways to bond with your spouse. Have date nights and invest in your marriage.

Lord, You said it is not good for man to be alone.

Lord, bless my spouse and I to be a great companion to one another.

I pray that my spouse and I will enjoy each other's company.

I bind up the spirit of loneliness, abandonment, and division in Jesus' name.

I pray that my spouse and I won't be disconnected from each other.

Lord, bless my spouse and I to connect emotionally, physically, and spiritually.

I bind up distractions when my spouse and I are spending time together.

I bind up any agents of Satan that will try to get between my spouse and I.

I pray that my spouse and I will miss each other when we aren't around each other.

Lord, I pray that my spouse and I will never be too busy for each other.

I pray that my spouse and I will show each other how important we are to each other.

I pray that my spouse and I can work on our purpose, destiny, business, or ministry together.

I bind up any single talk in my marriage.

I bind up any single mentality that will operate through my spouse and I.

I pray that my spouse and I will laugh and have fun together.

I pray that my spouse and I will satisfy each other's needs.

Lord, bless my spouse and I to find something that we enjoy doing together.

Lord, bless my spouse and I to build memories.

Lord, bless my spouse and I to become one flesh.

Lord, bless my spouse and I not to be selfish.

I pray that my spouse and I will be welcoming of each other.

I pray that my spouse and I will be glad to see each other.

I pray that my spouse and I will enjoy conversing with one another.

I bind up my spouse and I's attempt to punish each other if we are upset.

I pray that my spouse and I will be cheerful and pleasant to be around.

Lord, increase the intimacy in my marriage.

Lord, bless my spouse and I to pray with one another.

Lord, bless my spouse and I to try new things together.

Lord, bless my spouse and I to get out of debt.

Lord, bless my spouse and I to travel and date often.

Lord, bless my spouse and I financially so we can invest in our marriage.

Lord, bless my spouse and I to be best friends.

Lord, bless my spouse and I to be able to solve any problems that arise.

Lord, bless my spouse and I to eat our meals together.

Lord, bless my spouse and I to sleep in the same bed.

Lord, bless my spouse and I to be a positive reinforcement to each other.

I pray that my spouse and I will keep each other's interests.

I pray that my spouse and I will keep each other up so we can give each other eye candy.

I pray that my spouse and I will flirt and speak each other's love languages.

I pray that my spouse and I will be willing to do things that each other enjoys.

I bind up any arguing spirits in Jesus' name.

Lord, loose peace and love in my home in Jesus' name.

Lord, keep the love fresh between my spouse and I.

Lord, let my marriage be a great example of a Kingdom marriage.

Lord, bless my spouse and I to understand each other's needs.

Lord, whatever is broken in my marriage please fix it.

Lord, I bind up any distance in my marriage in Jesus' name.

I bind up divorce and separation in Jesus' name.

I bind up the fear of communication.

I bind up any demonic attacks on my marriage in Jesus' name.

DAY SIXTEEN

Spiritual

A SPIRITUAL CONNECTION IS AS powerful as a physical one. God is serious about us being equally yoked with our spouses. In the Bible, His children didn't believe in marrying people who served other gods because it could result in idolatry which occurred on multiple occasions. For instance, King Solomon started off serving God, but he had many foreign wives that brought their false beliefs into the palace. Solomon was influenced by them, and as a punishment, the Kingdom split into the Northern and Southern Kingdom (1 Kings 12). Also, we are warned not to be unequally yoked with unbelievers. It's stressful when one spouse is saved and the other isn't. A house divided against itself can't stand. We must pray and read the Bible with our spouses. Everything can't be carnal because our relationship with God will suffer. A family that prays together will definitely stay together. They will weather the storm and discern when there are demonic entities at work. Couples working together are a threat to the enemy's camp.

I decree that my spouse will be a person after God's own heart.

Spiritual

I decree that my spouse is saved and sanctified in Jesus' name.

I pray that my spouse will invest in their spiritual growth.

Lord, bless my spouse to come into alignment with Your will.

I decree that my spouse will come up spiritually in the name of Jesus.

I decree that my spouse will be on fire for the Lord Jesus Christ.

I decree that my spouse will be zealous about the things of God.

I decree that my spouse will have a burden for prayer and intercession.

I decree that my spouse will fast regularly.

I decree that my spouse will demonstrate the Kingdom of God.

I decree that my spouse will have strong discernment.

I decree that my spouse will lay hands on the sick and they will recover.

I decree that my spouse will hear the Lord's voice clearly.

I decree that my spouse will be sensitive to God's Spirit.

I decree that my spouse will love the Lord with all their heart, soul, and mind.

I decree that my spouse will be obedient to God's commands.

I decree that my spouse will be full of God's Word.

I decree that my spouse has the Wisdom of God in their life.

I decree that my spouse and I will pray together.

I decree that my spouse and I will read the Bible together.

I decree that my spouse and I will do couple's devotions to grow together.

I decree that my spouse and I will attend church together.

I decree that my spouse and I won't be divided about spiritual things.

I decree that my spouse has a real relationship with Jesus' Christ.

I decree that my spouse's footsteps are ordered by the Lord.

Spiritual

I decree that my spouse will do the work of an evangelist.

I decree that my spouse will preach the gospel fervently.

I decree that my spouse will never compromise or sin against God.

I decree that my spouse has the fear of the Lord in their heart.

I decree that my spouse is in love with the Father, Son, and the Holy Spirit.

I decree that my spouse will be holy as God is holy.

I decree that my spouse will worship the Lord in spirit and in truth.

I decree that my spouse be a godly example for our family.

I decree that my spouse will allow the Holy Spirit to flow through them.

I decree that my spouse is sharpened in the gifts of the Holy Spirit.

I decree that my spouse will not just be a hearer of the Word but a doer of the Word.

I decree that my spouse will walk in a spirit of excellence.

I pray that my spouse will study the Word of God to show themselves approved unto the Lord.

I pray that my spouse will be a good steward over the anointing on their life.

I pray that my spouse will crucify their flesh and die to self.

I pray that my spouse will never get caught up in false doctrine or beliefs.

Lord, deliver my spouse from anything that is not of You.

Lord, soften my spouse's heart for things of God.

Lord, bless my spouse never to have a seared conscience.

Lord, bless my spouse to be humble and a contrite heart.

Lord, bless my spouse never to neglect their time with You.

Lord, bless my spouse to be accountable to other godly people and me.

Lord, bless my spouse to submit to godly leadership.

Lord, bless my spouse and I to worship You together.

Spiritual

Lord, show my spouse their identity in You.

Lord, bless my spouse to walk in their purpose and destiny.

Lord, bless my spouse to stay hidden in Jesus Christ.

DAY SEVENTEEN

Healthy

WE ONLY GET ONE body in this life. Our lifestyle determines the wear and tear on it. If we eat bad foods, then we are at higher risk for certain diseases. When we practice risky behaviors such as adultery, homosexuality, drugs, etc., we can die prematurely because sin equals death. When we marry, it's not all about us. Our spouses need us and desire to spend a long life with us. If we are gluttonous, then we are selfish. It's not fair to our spouses if they have to bury us if we die prematurely due to unhealthiness. It is also not fair if we can't spend time with our spouses because we are always sick. Our bodies are the temple of the Holy Spirit. Also, our bodies belong to our spouses. Every time my husband has been sick, I've been concerned. He used to eat very unhealthy food and he was set in his ways. I prayed and fasted about it. Then one day, my husband approached me and said, "Babe, I will no longer eat ramen noodles, potato chips, ground beef, etc., but I want to start eating healthy." My prayers were answered and now my husband has embraced this new lifestyle change. He has been feeling great. If you don't make a lifestyle change for yourself, then do it for your family.

Healthy

I decree that my spouse is in good health in Jesus' name.

I decree that all will be well with my spouse and they will be in good health as their soul prospers.

Lord, burn up any hidden growths or tumors in my spouse's body in Jesus' name.

Lord, cancel any disease that is time-sensitive or appointed by the enemy for a certain date in Jesus' name.

I bind up heart disease off my spouse in the name of Jesus.

I bind up gluttony off my spouse in the name of Jesus.

I bind up any recurrent pain off my spouse's body in the name of Jesus.

I bind up strokes and high blood pressure off my spouse in the name of Jesus.

I bind up any cancer off my spouse in the name of Jesus.

I bind up any blood disorders off my spouse in the name of Jesus.

I bind up any diabetes off my spouse in the name of Jesus.

I bind up any skin disorders off my spouse in the name of Jesus.

I decree that by Jesus' stripes my spouse is healed.

I decree that Jesus took those thirty-nine lashes on the cross for my spouse's health and wellness.

Lord, if my spouse has any addictions to alcohol, break now in Jesus' name.

Lord, bless my spouse to have great mental health.

Lord, bless my spouse to have great emotional health.

Lord, break off any drug addictions that will try to attach to my spouse in the name of Jesus.

Lord, satisfy my spouse with a long life.

It doesn't matter what the doctor may have said concerning my spouse, I believe the report of the Lord.

Lord, anoint my spouse with Your healing Balm of Gilead.

I bind up any sickness and disease that is attached to my spouse in the name of Jesus.

I bind up any stubborn infirmities off my spouse in the name of Jesus.

Healthy

I decree that my spouse will never be a drunk in the name of Jesus.

I bind up any risky or dangerous behaviors off my spouse in the name of Jesus.

I bind up any demonic strongholds and demonic influence off my spouse in the name of Jesus.

Lord, if I pray a prayer of faith, my spouse will be made well.

I break any generational curses of sickness off my spouse's bloodline in the name of Jesus.

I bind up premature death off my spouse in the name of Jesus.

I prophesy that my spouse will have a long life in the name of Jesus.

Lord, if my spouse has any damage to any tissue or organs in their body, please restore, regenerate, and heal it now in the name of Jesus.

Lord, bless my spouse not to be negligent about their health.

Lord, bless my spouse to get regular checkups at the doctor.

Lord, if my spouse doesn't have health insurance, bless them financially in Jesus' name.

Lord, bless my spouse to make healthier lifestyle changes.

Lord, bless my spouse to eat healthier.

Lord, bless my spouse to exercise regularly.

Lord, bless my spouse to have a healthy body weight.

Lord, if my spouse is out of shape, bless them to get fit in Jesus' name.

Lord, bless my spouse to have great hygiene in Jesus' name.

Lord, bless my spouse to get all the nutrients and vitamins they need.

Lord, strengthen my spouse's immune system in Jesus' name.

Lord, protect my spouse from COVID-19 and any other deadly viruses in Jesus' name.

Lord, I bind up insomnia off my spouse in Jesus' name.

Lord, allow no plague to come near my spouse's dwelling.

Lord, protect my spouse from tragedies and any danger in Jesus' name.

Lord, bless my spouse to recognize that their body is the temple of the Holy Spirit.

I decree that my spouse will always be sexually faithful to me so they will never bring home sexually transmitted diseases in Jesus' name.

I bind up any depression and withdrawal from society off my spouse in the name of Jesus.

I decree that my spouse and I will love each other through sickness and health in the name of Jesus.

I bind up any chronic diseases off my spouse in the name of Jesus.

I decree that bad health will never be an issue or a hindrance for my spouse to do what the Lord is calling them to do.

I bind up any work injuries in the name of Jesus.

I decree that my spouse is healthy and strong and will be able to work a great job in Jesus' name.

DAY EIGHTEEN

Peaceful

GOD CALLS US TO be peacemakers. It's stressful to have a house full of drama where you have to constantly walk on eggshells. The enemy wants our house to be full of strife and division. However, Jesus Christ is the prince of peace. After a long stressful day, our spouses should come home to a safe haven. They might be going through warfare outside of the home and don't need it inside. Instead of fighting, decide to make peace. Sometimes I apologize first, even when I am not at fault. I surrender everything unto the Lord and He convicts my spouse. As a result, my husband always apologizes in return. We have to choose and fight our battles.

I decree that my spouse is a peacemaker and will be known as a son of God in Jesus' name.

I decree that my spouse will live peaceably with all men.

I decree that my spouse and I will have peace in our household in Jesus' name.

I decree that my spouse will confess when they are wrong and apologize.

I decree that my spouse will be quick to hear and slow to speak in Jesus' name.

I decree that my spouse will do whatever it takes to resolve any conflicts between us.

I decree that my spouse will not hold onto grudges.

I decree that my spouse will not allow the sun to go down on their wrath.

I decree that my spouse will not sin if they become angry.

I decree that my spouse and I won't argue all the time.

I decree that the presence of God dwells strongly in my house.

I decree that my spouse will renew their mind.

I decree that my spouse will let go of any malice, division, and strife in Jesus' name.

I decree that my spouse won't be worried or stressed out about things that are out of their control in Jesus' name.

I decree that my spouse will humble themselves and walk away from foolish conversations so things will never escalate.

Lord, keep watch over my spouse's mouth.

Lord, bless my spouse to yield to you so you can develop Christ-like characteristics in them.

Lord, season my spouse's speech with wisdom.

Lord, bless my spouse to discern which battles to fight.

Lord, bless my spouse to keep their mind on Jesus so they can have perfect peace.

Lord, give my spouse peace that surpasses all understanding.

Lord, be with my spouse and give them peace at all times.

Lord, bless the peace of God to rule in my spouse's heart.

Lord, bless my spouse to always be thankful.

I decree that my spouse is an overcomer.

I decree that my spouse will not allow their heart to be troubled.

Lord, bless my spouse to cast their cares upon You.

Peaceful

Lord, bless my spouse to get enough sleep at night.

I bind up any restlessness or anxiousness off my spouse in Jesus' name.

I decree that my spouse will not be afraid but trust in God.

Lord, bless my spouse to be joyful and cheerful to be around in the name of Jesus.

I decree Romans 15:13 that the God of hope will fill my spouse with joy and peace in believing, so that by the power of the Holy Spirit, they may abound in hope.

I decree Hebrews 12:14 that my spouse will strive for peace with everyone.

I decree Romans 8:6 that my spouse's mind is set on the Spirit, which is life and peace.

I decree 1 Peter 3:11 that my spouse will turn away from evil and do good.

I decree 1 Peter 3:11 that my spouse will seek peace and pursue it.

I decree Romans 5:1 over my spouse that they have been justified by faith and will have peace with God through our Lord Jesus Christ.

I decree Psalm 119:165 that my spouse will have great peace because they love God's law and nothing can make them stumble.

Lord, bless my spouse to reap a harvest of righteousness that is sown in peace.

Lord, bless my spouse to have the fruits of the Holy Spirit operating strongly in their life.

I decree Proverbs 16:7 that my spouse's ways pleases the Lord and their enemies will be at peace with them.

I decree that my spouse will not start arguments or have unforgiveness in their heart.

I decree that my spouse will go out of their way to show me loving-kindness in Jesus' name.

I decree that my spouse won't say or do things to purposely hurt my feelings.

I decree that my spouse won't be insensitive to my needs or feelings.

I decree that my spouse and I will enjoy each other daily.

I decree that my spouse and I will love and respect each other.

Peaceful

I decree that my spouse and I will make quality time for each other.

I decree that my spouse will walk in the Spirit so they don't fulfill the lust of the flesh.

DAY NINETEEN

Great Leader

❃

THERE IS NOTHING WORSE than the blind leading the blind. The husband must lead his family because he is called to be a priest of the home. God has set order and it is as follows: God is first. The husband is second. The wife is third. The man is the head of the wife. A wife must submit to her husband. When I married my husband, I had to submit to his leadership. I used to let my children eat anytime they wanted and play their games at the table. They would sit at the table for hours. When my husband came into our lives, he began to set order. He put rules into place, such as dinner time is at 5 pm and no devices at the table. At first, the children hated it; but they learned to listen. They no longer sat at the table for hours and we all bonded as a family. We are glad for the rules because things run smoothly and we are happy. If the husband isn't in place, keep praying because God can bring alignment in his life.

I decree that my spouse is a great leader.

I decree that the husband is the priesthood of his home.

Great Leader

I decree that my spouse will have integrity in Jesus' name.

I decree that the husband will love his wife as Christ loves the church.

I decree that my spouse will be able to delegate.

I decree that my spouse will have great communication skills.

I decree that my spouse will be well respected by others.

I decree that my spouse will be humble.

I decree that my spouse is innovative and hard-working.

I decree that my spouse will be honest.

I decree that my spouse will be a great listener.

I decree that my spouse will be confident in who God created them to be.

I decree that my spouse will be a visionary.

I decree that my spouse will have great problem-solving skills.

I decree that my spouse will motivate others.

I decree that my spouse and I will decide together when making major decisions.

I decree that my spouse will allow God to order their steps.

I decree that my spouse will seek God for His counsel and might.

I decree that my spouse will have a sound mind.

I decree that my spouse will be bold and stand up for righteousness.

I decree that my spouse will make the best decisions for our family.

I pray that my spouse will be an imitator of Jesus Christ.

I decree that my spouse will stay on the straight and narrow path.

I decree Psalms 23:3 that God will restore my spouse's soul and lead them in the paths of righteousness.

I decree 1 Timothy 4:12 over my spouse that they will set an example in speech, conduct, love, faith, and purity in Jesus' name.

I decree that my spouse will be an example to other believers.

Great Leader

I decree that my spouse will have the heart of a servant.

I decree that my spouse will have empathy and compassion for others.

I decree that my spouse has self-discipline.

I decree that my spouse will be emotionally stable.

I decree that my spouse will have great social skills.

I decree that my spouse will be productive in their assignments.

I decree that my spouse will be a great accountability partner.

I decree that my spouse is supportive.

I decree that my spouse is tech-savvy.

I decree that my spouse is faith-filled.

I decree that my spouse is optimistic.

I decree that my spouse trusts in the Lord.

I decree that my spouse has great time management skills.

I decree that my spouse has a great personality in Jesus' name.

Lord, bless my spouse with the gift of leadership.

Lord, bless my spouse to not compromise in their walk with You.

I decree that my spouse will never be bribed in Jesus' name.

I decree that my spouse will never be corrupt in Jesus' name.

I decree that my spouse will stay pure in God's sight.

I decree that my spouse will not grieve God's Spirit.

I decree that my spouse will never have scandals attached to their name.

I decree that my spouse is trustworthy.

Lord, bless my spouse with a teachable spirit.

DAY TWENTY

Go-getter

A GO-GETTER IS VERY AMBITIOUS and does what God sets to do in their hearts. When God gives me an idea, I run with it. I don't procrastinate but go forth by working hard to accomplish it. My husband gives me space and allows me to write my books. I also let him have room to execute his photography goals. I never want to hinder his goals because I want him to be all that he can be in life. I desire for God to open up doors that no one can shut. Together, my husband and I have done some great things in multimedia. God is the best creator, so He understands the realm of creativity. God has placed vision inside of us and we need Him to accomplish them. When things are too big or seem out of reach, God will help us to fulfill them.

I decree that my spouse will be a go-getter in Jesus' name.

I decree that wherever the Lord goes, my spouse will follow.

I decree that my spouse will obey God rather than man.

I decree my spouse is an achiever.

I decree that my spouse is a hearer and doer of God's word.

I decree that my spouse will not be a procrastinator.

I decree that my spouse will not be lazy in Jesus' name.

I decree that my spouse will make the most use of their time.

I decree that my spouse will achieve their dreams in Jesus' name.

I decree that my spouse will search out a matter and do research when new opportunities arise.

I decree that whatever my spouse's hands touch would prosper in Jesus' name.

I decree that my spouse will lack no good thing.

I decree that my spouse will walk in overflow.

I decree that my spouse's cup will run over.

I decree that my spouse will do things without grumbling or complaining.

I decree that my spouse will walk underneath an open Heaven.

I decree that God's favor will surround my spouse as a shield.

I decree that my spouse will never be put to shame.

No weapon formed against my spouse will prosper in Jesus' name.

I decree that my spouse will be a light in dark places.

I decree that the Glory of the Lord will shine upon my spouse.

I decree that people will glorify God because my spouse is doing great work.

I decree that my spouse will not quit when things get tough.

I decree that my spouse will overcome every challenge.

I decree that the hands of the diligent make it rich.

I decree that my spouse will have profit in their toil.

I decree that my spouse will do all things through Christ that strengthen them.

I decree that my spouse will commit their work to the Lord so their plans can be established.

I decree that my spouse will soar through adversity in Jesus' name.

I decree that my spouse will have perseverance in the name of Jesus.

I decree that my spouse will be resourceful in Jesus' name.

I decree that my spouse will not despise small beginnings.

I decree that my spouse will not get weary in well-doing.

I decree that my spouse will war over their prophecies in the name of Jesus.

I decree that my spouse will set their face like a flint.

I decree that my spouse will be zealous for the things of God.

I decree that whatever my spouse does, they will do it unto the Lord.

I decree that my spouse's hand will rule in Jesus' name.

I decree that my spouse will walk circumspectly.

I decree that my spouse will walk in a way that is worthy of the Lord.

Go-getter

I decree that my spouse is willing and obedient and will eat the good of the land.

I decree Jeremiah 29:11 over my spouse that God has great plans to bring them a blessed future and hope.

Lord, straighten every crooked path in my spouse's life.

Lord, make every rough place smooth in my spouse's life.

Lord, open up doors for my spouse that no man can shut.

Lord, let the gifts on my spouse's life make room for them and bring them into the presence of great men.

I bind up excuse-making off my spouse.

I pray that my spouse will have the gift of the word of wisdom.

I decree that my spouse will be in sync with the timing of God.

I decree that my spouse will be like the sons of Issachar.

I decree that my spouse's zeal will line up with God's will.

DAY TWENTY ONE

Trusting

TRUST INVOLVES BEING VULNERABLE with someone and letting the walls down. We must realize that our spouses are for us and want the best for us. They aren't against us, so we can trust them. There should be no secrets in our marriage. I never want to make my husband feel insecure. I have no codes, passwords, or emails that he doesn't know about. I leave my phone unlocked. I have nothing to hide. My husband does the same thing. We don't leave any room for the devil. It's stressful double-checking behind someone. God wants to bring healing to our hearts and deliver us from any insecurities so we can enjoy the marriage he blessed us with.

Lord bless my spouse to trust You with their whole heart, soul, and mind.

Lord, bless my spouse to put their trust in You instead of material things.

Lord, bless my spouse and I to trust one another.

Trusting

I bind up any demonic attacks off my marriage in Jesus' name.

I decree Proverbs 3:5 over my spouse that they will trust in the Lord with all their heart and lean not on their own understanding.

I decree Psalm 56:3 over my spouse that when they are afraid, they will put their trust in God.

I decree Psalm 56:4 over my spouse that will not be afraid of flesh or people.

I decree that my spouse will trust God's plans for their life.

Lord, baptize my spouse in Your love because perfect love casts out fear.

Lord, perfect my spouse in Your love because fear has to do with punishment.

I decree Psalm 37:5 that my spouse will commit their way to You, trust You, so You can act on their behalf.

Lord, bless my spouse never to get ahead of You.

Lord, bless my spouse to be still and know that You are God.

I decree that my spouse will trust in God's steadfast love.

I decree that whatever my spouse asks in prayer, they will receive it.

I decree that my spouse will have perfect peace because their minds is stayed on God.

I decree that my spouse will trust in the Lord forever because He is an everlasting rock.

I decree Psalm 9:10 that the Lord will never forsake my spouse because they seek Him.

I decree that my spouse will not be anxious about anything.

Lord, make my spouse's paths straight.

I decree Psalm 118:8 that it is better to take refuge in the Lord than to trust in man.

I decree that my spouse is blessed because they trust in the Lord.

I decree that my spouse is like a tree planted by water and their leaves will not wither.

Lord, refresh my spouse and bless them with strength.

Lord, bless my spouse and I to have security in each other.

Lord, bless my spouse and I to believe in Your promises.

Trusting

I bind up jealousy in my marriage in Jesus' name.

I bind up disappointments from my marriage in the name of Jesus.

I decree that my spouse will be true to their word and through with their actions.

I decree that my spouse will have great communication with others in the name of Jesus.

Lord, build up the trust in my marriage.

Lord, restore any fragmented pieces in my marriage.

Lord, bless my spouse to think before they act in Jesus' name.

Lord, place a hedge of protection around my marriage in Jesus' name.

Lord, bless my spouse and I to grow closer.

Lord, bless my spouse and I to honor and respect one another in Jesus' name.

I bind up betrayal, lies, or doubts off my marriage in Jesus' name.

Lord, bless my spouse to be fully committed to our marriage.

Lord, bless my spouse to have godly character.

Lord, bless my spouse to disassociate with any person that is on assignment to destroy our marriage.

Lord, bless my spouse to have integrity and do the right thing.

Lord, shield my spouse from any seductress or seducer in Jesus' name.

Lord, bless my spouse and I to only have eyes for each other.

Lord, bless my spouse and I to know each other's passwords and information.

I bind up secrets in my marriage in Jesus' name.

Lord, remove the wrong people out of my spouse's path.

I bind up adultery and lust in the name of Jesus.

I bind up any division in the name of Jesus.

DAY TWENTY TWO

Faithful

FAITHFULNESS IS BEING LOYAL and committed to our spouses. We only have eyes for them and come home to them every night. We place no other people before them. When my husband and I married, we blocked and deleted people interested in us or a threat to our relationship. Some women got mad at my husband and started stalking us on social media. They would send us nasty messages trying to curse us. Some men unfriended me and stopped conversing with me. Not everyone was happy with my husband and me, so we knew they had an ulterior motive. As God is faithful to us, we should be faithful to our spouses because our marriage is a covenant relationship.

I decree that my spouse and I will be faithful to one another in Jesus' name.

I decree that my spouse and I will cherish one another.

I decree that my spouse and I will guard one another's hearts.

I decree that my spouse and I will esteem each other highly.

I pray that my spouse and I will be honest with each other.

I pray that my spouse and I will honor our marital vows.

Lord, bless my spouse and I to resolve any conflict.

Lord, bless my marriage to be built on the solid rock of Jesus Christ.

I decree my marriage is solid and unshakeable in Jesus' name.

I pray that my spouse and I will never cheat on each other.

I pray that my spouse and I will make each other a top priority.

I pray that my spouse and I will respect each other.

Lord, remove any insecurities out of my marriage in Jesus' name.

Lord, bless my spouse and I to build new memories together.

Lord remove any doubts in our minds about the love my spouse and I have for each other.

I bind up any single mentality in the name of Jesus.

I bind up fights and arguments in my marriage in the name of Jesus.

Lord, bless my spouse and I to be accountable in the name of Jesus.

I pray that my spouse and I will never stress each other out.

I decree that my spouse and I will not rub each other the wrong way.

I pray that my spouse and I will make the necessary sacrifices to be a successful team.

I bind up my spouse and I from having any emotional affairs with other people.

I pray that my spouse and I will have great intimacy in Jesus' name.

Lord, bless my spouse and I to have loving gestures.

Lord, bless my spouse and I to show each other affection.

Lord, keep the bond strong between my spouse and I.

Lord, bless my spouse and I to flirt and whisper sweet nothings to each other daily.

Lord, bless my spouse and I to affirm each other.

Lord, keep the passion strong in my marriage.

I bind up my spouse and I doing hurtful things to see each other's reaction in Jesus' name.

I bind up any fiction in the name of Jesus.

I bind up the appearance of wrongdoing in Jesus' name.

I pray that my spouse and I won't play with fire.

I pray that my spouse and I won't entertain people with wrong motives.

I pray that my spouse and I will be happily married in Jesus' name.

I bind up any fantasies that my spouse and I will have about other people.

I bind up silly crushes that my spouse and I may have.

Lord, bless my spouse and I to cast down every vain imagination.

Lord, bless my spouse and I to cast down sinful thoughts.

Lord, renew my spouse's and my minds in Jesus' name.

Lord, allow any doors to past relationships that my spouse and I had to remain closed.

I decree that my spouse and I will always shun evil and dismiss any person that is attracted to us.

Lord, bless my spouse and I to do more things together in Jesus' name.

Lord, remove the wrong people out of my spouse's and my life in Jesus' name.

I pray that my spouse and I won't complain when we are doing things for one another.

Lord, I pray that the plans my spouse and I made will come into fruition in Jesus' name.

Lord, I pray that my spouse and I will have open communication and not take offense when we are expressing our feelings.

Lord, bless my spouse and I to fight for our marriage and endure to the end in Jesus' name.

DAY TWENTY THREE

Committed

WHEN WE ARE COMMITTED to our spouse, we honor our marital vows. We treat our marriages differently than we would in a girlfriend or boyfriend relationship. We can't break things off when we get mad. We must stick it out. When my spouse and I disagree, we come back later and resolve things before the sun goes down on our wrath. We must guard our marriages and not allow anything to get between our spouses and us. We can't take everyone's advice because some will tell us to divorce our spouses. We must fight for our marriages and realize that some people want what we have. Love your spouse and treat them right unto God. Keep your heart pure so you can easily let things go and be pleasing in God's sight.

Lord, bless my spouse and I to be committed to each other.

Lord, bless my spouse and I to love each other in deeds not just in words.

Lord, bless my spouse and I to be loyal to each other.

Lord, bless my spouse and I to have romantic gestures and desire each other.

Lord, bless my spouse and I to respect and appreciate each other.

Lord, bless my spouse and I to be honest with each other.

Lord, bless my spouse and I to be trusting and empathetic towards each other.

Lord, bless my spouse and I to work together as a team and not compromise.

I pray that when my spouse and I disagree, it will be in a respectful way.

Lord, bless my spouse and I to pray with one another.

Lord, bless my spouse and I to submit to one another with a sincere heart.

I pray that my spouse and I will never neglect one another.

Lord, bless my spouse and I to encourage one another.

Lord, bless my spouse and I to always sleep in the same bed.

I bind up living two separate lives in Jesus' name.

I bind up any covenant breaking spirits in Jesus' name.

Lord, bless my spouse to be fully committed to You so they can be committed to me.

Lord, bless my spouse and I spend the rest of our lives making each other happy.

Lord bless my spouse and I to be dedicated to each other.

I bind up selfish motives in Jesus' name.

Lord bless my spouse and I to love each other despite our flaws.

Lord bless my spouse and I to overcome challenges in Jesus' name.

Lord bless my spouse and I to be loving and kind to each other.

I decree for better or for worse over my spouse in Jesus' name.

Lord, place a hedge of protection around my marriage in Jesus' name.

I plead the blood of Jesus upon my marriage in Jesus' name.

Lord, bless my spouse and I to enjoy one another's company.

Lord, bless my marriage to be healthy in Jesus' name.

Lord, bless my spouse and I to take care of each other in sickness.

Lord, remove any unforgiveness out of my spouse's and my heart.

Love covers a multitude of sins.

Lord, bless my spouse and I to be able to celebrate with each other.

Lord, bless my spouse and I to have synergy.

Lord, bless my spouse and I to serve You together.

Lord, bless my spouse and I with a great sex life in the name of Jesus.

Lord, bless my spouse and I to invest in our marriage.

Lord, when my spouse and I mess up, allow us to apologize.

Lord, bless my spouse and I to keep people out of our marriage.

Lord, strengthen the unity between my spouse and I as we transition through different seasons.

Lord, bless my spouse and I to weather the storms.

Lord, bless my spouse and I to place safety nets around our marriage.

I decree that the Lord will order my spouse's and my steps.

I decree that my spouse's and my feet will never stumble.

Lord, bless my spouse and I with discernment so we won't be a prey to the enemy.

Lord, bless my spouse and I to fight for our marriage daily.

Lord, keep the passion strong in my marriage.

Lord, bless my spouse and I to be best friends.

I bind up temptation and distractions in Jesus' name.

Lord, bless my spouse and I to always spend time together.

DAY TWENTY FOUR

Right Alignment with God

*I*F WE AREN'T IN right alignment with God, then things will be a mess in our lives. If we don't love the Lord properly, then we won't be able to love our spouses correctly. God makes us a better person: father, mother, son, daughter, sister, brother, husband, wife, etc. We can love, honor, and respect our spouses to glorify God. God can use our marriage as an example of a Kingdom marriage. If my husband and I had met years before we did, things wouldn't have worked. He was a womanizer and alcoholic. I was self-centered, career-focused, scorned, and had an attitude problem. God saved and transformed us. We are new creatures in Christ and our old character no longer exists. If your spouse is not in right standing with God, keep believing and praying. Things will turn around.

Lord, bless my spouse to be in right alignment with You.

Lord, bless my spouse to have a burden for prayer and intercession.

I bind up any demonic influence on my spouse's mind in Jesus' name.

Lord, bless my spouse to speak life over me in Jesus' name.

Lord, bless my spouse to be a person after Your heart.

Lord, bless my spouse to be in sync with Your Spirit.

Lord, order my spouse's steps in Jesus' name.

Lord, bless my spouse to be a worshipper in Jesus' name.

Lord, bless my spouse to love You with their whole heart.

Lord, strengthen my spouse's faith walk.

Lord, bless my spouse to be transformed more into the image of Jesus Christ.

Lord, bless my spouse to be an imitator of Jesus Christ.

Lord, bless my spouse to be confident in You.

Lord, bless my spouse to be a glory carrier in Jesus' name.

Lord, bless my spouse to grow deeper in You.

Right Alignment with God

Lord, use my spouse in signs, wonders, and miracles in Jesus' name.

Lord, bless my spouse to follow Your commandments.

Lord, bless my spouse to always obey You even when they are out of their comfort zone.

Lord, bless my spouse to read the Bible daily.

Lord, bless my spouse to demonstrate Your power.

Lord, bless my spouse to delight themselves in You.

Lord, bless my spouse to be rooted and grounded in You.

Lord, bless my spouse to be planted in the house of the Lord,

Lord, bless my spouse to be baptized with Your fire.

Lord, deliver my spouse from any demonic strongholds in Jesus' name.

Lord, bless my spouse to prioritize their time with You.

Lord, bless my spouse to give You their first fruits.

Lord, bless my spouse to stay abiding in You so they can produce great fruit.

Lord, bless my spouse to meditate on Your Word.

Lord, bless my spouse to renew their mind.

Lord, bless my spouse with great faith.

Lord, bless the prophecies concerning my spouse to come to pass.

Lord, bless my spouse to rest in You.

Lord, I decree Romans 12:2 over my spouse that they won't be conformed to this world but be transformed by the renewing of their minds so that by testing, they may discern the perfect will of God.

I decree Jeremiah 29:11 over my spouse that the Lord has a great future and hope for them.

I decree that my spouse will present their bodies as a living sacrifice.

I decree Matthew 5:16 over my spouse that people may see their great works and glorify the Lord.

Lord, bless my spouse not to be double minded in Jesus' name.

Lord, bless my spouse to walk in a manner worthy of their calling.

Lord, bless my spouse to have a pure heart in Your sight.

Lord, bless my spouse with wisdom so they can always do the right thing.

Lord, bless my spouse to be ready in season and out of season.

I decree Colossians 3:23 that whatever my spouse does, it will be unto the Lord.

I pray that my spouse will be a good steward over what You have given them.

I pray that my spouse will radiate the love of God.

I pray that my spouse will not be wise in their own eyes but to turn away from evil.

I pray that my spouse's mind will not be set on the flesh because it's hostile to God.

Lord, let Your will be done in my spouse's life.

DAY TWENTY FIVE

Humble

WHEN OUR SPOUSES ARE humble, they will be blessed and exalted in God's sight. Pride comes before destruction. Nabal was very foolish and as a result, he lost his life due to his pride (1 Samuel 25). Nabal's actions endangered his family and staff. It's difficult communicating or being with a prideful person. God can transform a hard heart and soften it. My husband and I used to struggle with pride, but God knows how to humble us. After the storm, he was a different man and I was a different woman. He saw a lot of his mistakes and surrendered everything to God. Our marriage has been better. If you or your spouse have pride, humble yourself in God's sight. It is better to humble ourselves before God does.

Lord, bless my spouse to be humble in Jesus' name.

Lord, bless my spouse to have a teachable spirit in the name of Jesus.

I pray that my spouse never steals God's glory.

Humble

Lord, you oppose the proud but give grace unto the humble.

I decree James 4:10 over my spouse that they will humble themselves before the Lord and He will exalt them.

I pray that my spouse will not be stubborn in Jesus' name.

I pray that my spouse will never be put to shame.

I pray Colossians 3:12 over my spouse that they will have a compassionate heart, kindness, humility, meekness, and patience,

I pray Ephesians 4:2 over my spouse with all humility and gentleness with patience and bearing with one another in love.

I pray Philippians 2:3 that my spouse will do nothing from rivalry or conceit.

I pray Philippians 2:3 over my spouse that they will count others more significant than themselves.

I bind up the selfishness off my spouse in Jesus' name.

Lord, satisfy my spouse with long life in Jesus' name.

Lord, place the spirit of honor upon my spouse in Jesus' name.

Lord, loose purity over my spouse.

I decree Proverbs 15:33 over my spouse that the fear of the Lord is instruction in wisdom, and humility comes before honor.

Lord, bless my spouse not to become defensive or argumentative.

Lord, bless my spouse to trust You to fight their battles.

Lord, bless my spouse not to be boastful in themselves.

I decree 1 Peter 5:5 that my spouse will clothe themself in humility.

Lord, bless my spouse to be meek.

Lord bless my spouse to have a servant's heart.

I pray that my spouse will be yielded to You.

Lord, bless my spouse to surrender all unto You.

Lord, let my spouse be imitators of Jesus.

Lord, let my spouse be an ambassador of Jesus Christ.

Lord, bless my spouse to always point people back to Jesus.

Lord, bless my spouse to always repent if they mess up.

Humble

Lord, bless my spouse to be quick to listen and slow to speak.

Lord, bless my spouse to receive godly counsel from me.

Lord, bless my spouse to realize that I am not their enemy.

Lord, bless my spouse to fast and pray regularly in Jesus' name.

I pray that my spouse will rejoice when others are promoted, praised, or honored.

I decree that the enemy will never use my spouse against me.

I bind up the spirit of sabotage off my spouse in Jesus' name.

I decree that my spouse will not be wise in their own eyes.

I decree that my spouse will trust in the Lord and not their own hearts because it's deceitful above all things.

Lord, keep my spouse from falling into the enemy's traps.

Lord, give my spouse the fear of the Lord in their hearts.

Lord, bless my spouse to be devoted unto You.

Lord, bless my spouse to have the right heart posture before You.

I pray that my spouse will draw nigh to God.

I pray that my spouse will use their members as instruments of righteousness.

Lord, bless my spouse to speak life out of their mouths in Jesus' name.

DAY TWENTY SIX

Wisdom

HAVING WISDOM IS BEING knowledgeable and having good judgment. When we have God's wisdom, we make better choices and stop repeating the same mistakes. Having wisdom allows us to think before we act and consider the consequences. When we use good judgment, we guard the anointing and our marriages. We put boundaries in place with the opposite sex. We don't give people any room to gossip. A part of wisdom is building what the Lord has given you. When my husband and I married, we truly had nothing. We both were starting over in life. We lived in the country and had all kinds of pests. Eventually, we worked on our credit and moved into a better place for our family. It's amazing to look back and see the hand of the Lord increase us. God can give you wisdom for your marriage.

Lord, bless my spouse with godly wisdom.

I pray that my spouse won't be wise in their own eyes.

Lord, bless my spouse to be teachable.

Lord, bless my spouse to walk circumspectly.

I decree Proverbs 1:7 over my spouse that they will have the fear of the Lord, which is the beginning of knowledge.

Lord, bless my spouse to seek Your face so they will stand in Your counsel.

Lord, impart into my spouse the Word of wisdom so they will know how to build in life.

Lord, bless my spouse to always consider the costs before they act.

I decree Colossians 3:16 over my spouse that the word of Christ will dwell in them richly.

I decree that my spouse will give godly advice to others.

I decree that my spouse is a person devoted to the Word and prayer.

I decree Proverbs 18:15 over my spouse that their ears are wise and seek knowledge.

Lord, bless my spouse not to give full vent to their spirit but keep silent as You fight their battles.

Wisdom

I decree Luke 21:15 over my spouse that you will give them a mouth and wisdom which none of their adversaries will be able to refute.

Lord, bless my spouse with financial wisdom.

Lord, bless my spouse to be wise at the workplace.

Lord, bless my spouse to make the best decisions for our family.

Lord, shield my spouse from destruction.

I decree James 3:13 over my spouse that they will have good conduct and show their works in meekness of wisdom.

I decree Proverbs 14:8 over my spouse that they will have the wisdom of the prudent to discern their way.

I bind up any foolishness that would try to attach itself to my spouse.

I bind up the spirit of sabotage off my marriage in the name of Jesus.

I bind up any selfish behaviors off my spouse in the name of Jesus.

I decree that my spouse will be patient with me.

I decree that my spouse will appreciate me.

I decree that my spouse will have rule over their spirit.

I decree that my spouse will extend their loving kindness towards me.

I decree that my spouse is truthful.

I decree that my spouse will not be harsh or cold towards me.

I decree that my spouse will be gentle and compassionate towards me.

I decree that my spouse will go above and beyond to invest in our marriage.

I decree that my spouse is a peacemaker in Jesus' name.

I decree that my spouse and I will live in harmony.

I decree that my spouse will never tear down their own house.

I decree that my spouse will take care of themselves.

I decree that my spouse will eat healthy and exercise.

Wisdom

I decree that my spouse won't partake in destructive behaviors.

I decree that my spouse will never allow someone to get between us.

I decree that my spouse will renew their mind daily.

I decree that my spouse will allow God to create in them a pure heart.

Lord, guard my spouse's ears against ungodly counsel.

Lord, guard my spouse's eye gates that they will set no unworthy thing before it.

Lord, bless my spouse to stay on fire for You.

Lord, bless my spouse to be a great ambassador of Jesus Christ.

Lord, bless my spouse to be a great leader and role model to our family.

I bind up the devil from trying to use my spouse in Jesus' name.

DAY TWENTY SEVEN

Trail Blazer

When you are a trailblazer, you do things that no one in your family might have done or you open up doors for others. I was the first college graduate in my family and my sisters were inspired to go. My husband was the first in his family to become a photographer and now has several cousins following in his footsteps. We are putting our skills together to advance God's kingdom. My husband and I work hard to leave a legacy for our children. We know that God put us together for a reason. We have so much work to do together. God can use you and your spouse to do great exploits. Together you guys are a power team.

I decree that my spouse is a trailblazer in Jesus' name.

I decree that my spouse is a pioneer.

I decree that my spouse will set trends.

I decree that my spouse will break records.

I decree that my spouse will pave the way for others.

I decree that my spouse will have influence in Jesus' name.

I decree that my spouse will have favor with God and favor with man.

I decree that my spouse is innovative.

I decree that my spouse will implement those God ideas into fruition.

Lord, bless my spouse with strategies to win in life.

Lord, bless my spouse with inspiration to complete their god given assignment.

Lord, bless my spouse to motivate others to walk in their purpose.

Lord, anoint my spouse in their craft and set them apart for Your glory.

Lord, open up doors for my spouse that no one can shut.

Lord, give my spouse an anointing to lead.

Lord, bless my spouse to hear Your voice.

Lord, bless my spouse to be in sync with Your timing.

Lord, bless my spouse to be creative and do something this generation has never seen.

Lord, bless my spouse's gifts to make room for them.

Lord, prosper my spouse's hands.

Lord, give my spouse the power to generate wealth.

Lord, open up new streams of income for my spouse.

Lord, show my spouse who they can trust.

Lord, bless my spouse to be a problem solver.

Lord, bless my spouse to think outside of the box.

Lord, bless my spouse to be a hard worker.

Lord, increase my spouse.

Lord, bless my spouse to have great time management skills.

Lord, bless my spouse to be organized.

Lord, bless my spouse to be humble.

I pray that my spouse will never be intimidated by those after them.

Lord, bless my spouse with revelation.

Lord, bless my spouse with a Rhema word.

I decree that my spouse is the salt of the earth.

I decree that my spouse is the light of the world.

I decree that my spouse will not lose their saltiness.

I decree that my spouse will be bold as the lion of Judah.

I decree that my spouse will set their face like a flint.

Lord, show my spouse how to war over their prophecies.

Lord, bless my spouse to fast regularly.

Lord, bless my spouse to obey You even when it's out of their comfort zones.

Lord, bless my spouse to take up their cross daily and follow You.

I pray that my spouse will be courageous.

I pray that my spouse will empower others to succeed.

Lord, send divine connections for my spouse.

Lord, protect my spouse from any harm or danger.

I decree that my spouse will carry the conviction of the Lord.

I decree that my spouse will be an oracle for God.

Lord, strengthen my spouse's faith.

DAY TWENTY EIGHT

Confident

GOD HAS PLACED GIFTS in each of us and we must be confident of His ability that we can do great things. My husband and I do what we are anointed to do confidently. We know that we are human, but with the Lord, we can do supernatural things. God puts the supernatural in our natural. God anointed my husband for photography and me for writing. Together we create some awesome media projects and help others build their brand. God gets the glory out of what we are doing and we make sure everyone knows it. Don't doubt who God created you or your spouse to be. There is an anointing present on your spouse and your life. Walk in it.

I decree that my spouse will be confident.

I decree that my spouse is sexy and anointed.

I decree that my spouse knows who they are in the Lord Jesus Christ.

I decree that my spouse will stand firm in the Lord and the power of His might.

I decree that the Lord is my spouse's confidence and will keep their feet from being caught.

I decree that my spouse will put their confidence in God and not material things.

I decree that my spouse will never be jealous of anyone.

I bind up any insecurity off my spouse in Jesus' name.

I decree that my marriage is built upon the solid rock of Jesus Christ.

I bind up any invisible walls that my spouse and I have up in Jesus' name.

I decree that the trust in my marriage is strong in Jesus' name.

I decree that my spouse looks good, smells good, and feels good about themselves in Jesus' name.

I decree that my spouse and I won't be afraid to be vulnerable with each other.

I bind up any secrets in my marriages in Jesus' name.

I decree that my spouse and I know each other's passwords or account information.

I decree that my spouse and I will be upfront with each other.

I decree that my spouse and I will have fun with each other.

I decree that my spouse and I will overcome temptation in Jesus' name.

I decree that my spouse and I will close the door to our past in Jesus' name.

I decree that my spouse and I will remove any toxic people from our lives.

I decree that my spouse and I will work out any issues in Jesus' name.

I decree that my spouse and I won't bring any emotional baggage into our marriage.

I decree that my spouse and I will show each other off to the world in Jesus' name.

I decree that my spouse and I won't compare our relationships to others.

I decree that my spouse is full of faith.

I decree that my spouse is confident in getting results in prayer.

Lord, keep the passion and excitement strong in my marriage in Jesus' name.

Lord, bless my spouse and I to be focused on building our relationship.

Lord, bless my spouse and I to be confident in our God-given assignment.

I bind up any anxiety and stress that will try to overwhelm my spouse and I.

I bind up any double mindedness off my spouse and I in Jesus' name.

Lord, bless my spouse and I to be best friends.

I decree that my spouse will not throw away their confidence because it has a great reward.

Lord, bless my spouse to persevere so they can receive the promises You have for them.

I decree that my spouse will never do something that will hurt our relationship.

I bind up low self-esteem off my spouse in Jesus' name.

Confident

I bind up depression off my spouse in Jesus' name.

I decree that my spouse and I are happily married.

I pray that my spouse will confidently finish any task that they start.

I pray that my spouse won't lose confidence when things don't work out as planned.

I decree that my spouse will keep on going, pressing, asking, and seeking.

I decree that the Lord is my spouse's helper.

I decree that my spouse is unwavering in their faith.

I decree that my spouse will be victorious.

I decree Philippians 4:13 over my spouse that they can do all things through Christ who strengthens them.

I decree that my spouse will rise above every challenge in Jesus' name.

I decree that my spouse will accomplish anything that they set their minds on.

I decree that my spouse will do the right thing always and be in right standing with the Lord.

DAY TWENTY NINE

Debt Free

Having financial problems can put a strain on a marriage. Instead of dating, traveling, having nice stuff, the money for the family has to go elsewhere. Many couples divorce over finances. However, God can make a way. When my husband and I went through a wilderness season, the money was tight. We had debt accumulating and didn't know how to pay the bills at times. The only thing that we did know was that God would provide and He did. My husband had medical bills and I had legal fees and student loans. Over time, God has allowed us to pay off debt even in the COVID-19 pandemic. You and your spouse can overcome any challenge. Pray for a strategy to pay off debt and watch the Lord work.

Lord, bless my spouse and I with a supernatural debt elimination.

Lord, bless my spouse and I to pay off credit card bills.

Lord, bless my spouse and I to pay off medical bills.

Lord, bless my spouse and I to pay off any equipment.

Lord, bless my spouse and I to pay off any legal debt.

Lord, bless my spouse and I to pay off any child support.

Lord, bless my spouse and I to pay off our home and car early.

Lord, bless my spouse and I to pay off any taxes that we owe.

Lord, bless my spouse and I to pay off any student loans.

Lord, bless my spouse and I own the deed to land and any property.

Lord, close any holes in my spouse's and my pockets in Jesus' name.

Lord, bless my spouse and my pockets to be fat in Jesus' name.

Lord, increase my spouse and my credit scores in Jesus' name.

Lord, bless my spouse and I to pay all our bills on time.

Lord, bless my spouse and I with strategies to pay off debt.

Lord, increase my spouse and I in every way.

Lord, bless my spouse and I to walk in abundance in Jesus' name.

Lord, let my spouse and I's cup overflow in Jesus' name.

I decree that wealth and riches will be in my house in Jesus' name.

I decree that my spouse and I will owe nothing to no one except to love them.

I decree that my spouse and I are rich in every area of our lives.

I decree that my spouse and I will have integrity and pay back what we owe.

I bind up any stress that will try to attach to my spouse and I.

Lord, replenish any money supernaturally that we spent on bills.

Lord, bless my spouse and I to provide for our family.

Lord, bless my spouse and I to walk underneath an open heaven.

Lord, bless my spouse and I to leave an inheritance to our children's children.

I decree Matthew 6:33 that my spouse will seek first the kingdom of God and His righteousness, and all these things will be added to you.

Lord, open up to my spouse Your good treasury.

Lord, send rain upon my spouse's land in due season.

Lord, bless the work of our spouse's hand.

I decree that my spouse will lend to many nations and not borrow.

I decree that my spouse will be faithful in the little so they can be a ruler over much.

I decree that my spouse is above and never beneath.

I decree that my spouse and I will abound with blessings.

I decree that my spouse is blessed coming in and coming out.

I decree that my spouse is blessed in the city and the country.

I decree that my spouse is the head and not the tail.

I decree that my spouse and I will honor the Lord with our wealth and the first fruits of all our produce.

Debt Free

Lord, break the curse of poverty off my spouse and I.

Lord, loose generational blessings upon my spouse and I.

I bind up lack off my spouse in Jesus' name.

I decree that my spouse and I will have more than enough in Jesus' name.

I decree that our visions will be fully funded without us going into debt in Jesus' name.

I decree that God will supply my spouse's and my needs according to the riches in Christ Jesus.

I decree Proverbs 10:22 over my spouse that the blessings of the Lord will make them rich and add no sorrow with it.

Lord, bless my spouse to reap an abundant harvest.

I decree Matthew 6:12 that God will forgive our debts as we have forgiven our debtors.

Lord, bless my spouse and I to have money in the bank.

DAY THIRTY

Mentally Stable

THE ENEMY ATTACKS US in the soulish realm, such as the mind, will, and emotions. The enemy can cause us to make accusations or things that aren't even true. If we listen to the devil's lies, we will think the worst. We must get delivered, so we don't bring any baggage into our marriages. Before I remarried, I had to heal from a divorce and I knew I was ready to move on when I stopped bringing up my ex. My husband is nothing like my children's father. My husband had to heal as well. He embraced singleness for many years. We constantly renew our minds so we can have God's best for our lives. God's plans for our lives are to prosper us and give us a future.

Lord, bless my spouse to be mentally stable in Jesus' name.

Lord, I bind up double mindedness off my spouse.

I bind up any schizophrenia off my spouse in Jesus' name.

I bind up any bipolar disorder off my spouse in Jesus' name.

Mentally Stable

Lord, bless my spouse with a sound mind in Jesus' name.

Lord, bless my spouse to renew their mind daily.

I decree that my spouse will not be conformed to this world but be transformed by the renewing of their mind.

I decree that my spouse will cast down every high thought and imagination that exalts itself against the knowledge of Jesus Christ.

I bind up any demonic chatter coming against my spouse's mind.

I bind up any accusation that the enemy will try to whisper to my spouse.

I bind up any lie that the enemy has told my spouse in Jesus' name.

I decree that my spouse will set their minds on the spirit, which is life and peace.

I pray that my spouse will never come into agreement with Satan's deception.

I decree that my spouse will have perfect peace because their mind is stayed on Jesus.

I bind up anxiousness off my spouse.

I decree that the same mind that was in Jesus' Christ is also in me.

I decree that my spouse will be sober minded and vigilant because the adversary, the devil, seeks to destroy them like a roaring lion.

I bind up any trust issues out of my marriage.

I decree that my spouse will not be paranoid for any reason.

I decree that my spouse will be optimistic in Jesus' name.

I decree Colossians 3:2 that my spouse will set their minds on things that are above and not the things on the earth.

Lord, silence the accuser of the brethren in Jesus' name.

I decree that every seed that my Heavenly Father has not planted, be uprooted now in Jesus' name.

I decree that my spouse will not entertain any demonic thoughts.

I decree that my spouse's thoughts are pleasing in the Lord's sight.

I decree that my spouse is a new creature in Christ and the old has passed away.

Mentally Stable

I decree that my spouse will meditate on God's precepts and fix their eyes upon His ways.

I decree that my spouse will fix their mind on whatever is true, honorable, just, pure, lovely, commendable, excellence, and praise worthy.

I decree that my spouse will meditate on the Bible day and night so they can make their way prosperous and have good success.

Lord, search my spouse's mind and correct them if something is grievous to You.

I pray that my spouse will love the Lord with their whole soul and mind.

I decree James 4:7 over my spouse that they will submit to God, resist the devil and he will flee.

Lord, break any strongholds in my spouse's mind.

Lord, loose purity over my spouse's mind.

Lord, deliver my spouse from any traumatic experiences in Jesus' name.

Lord, heal any fragmented areas of my spouse's life.

I bind up the spirit of abandonment that will try to tell my spouse that I will leave them.

I bind up any false reality that will try to deceive my spouse.

Lord, strengthen my spouse as they receive deliverance.

Lord, bless my spouse to yield to You.

I bind up the spirit of self-sabotage in Jesus' name.

I decree that my spouse won't do things that they will later regret.

I decree that my spouse won't jump to conclusions but always find out the truth.

I decree that my spouse will have self-control.

I decree that my spouse won't take out their anger in me.

About The Author

KIMBERLY MOSES STARTED OFF her ministry as Kimberly Hargraves. She is highly sought after as a prophetic voice, intercessor and prolific author. There is no doubt that she has a global mandate on her life to serve the nations of the world by spreading the Gospel of Jesus Christ. She has a quickly expanding worldwide healing and deliverance ministry. Kimberly Moses wears many hats to fulfill the call God has placed on her life as an entrepreneur over several businesses including her own personal brand Rejoice Essentials which promotes the Gospel of Jesus Christ.

She also serves as a life coach and mentor to many women. She is also the loving mother of two wonderful children. She is married to Tron. Kimberly has dedicated her life to the work of ministry and to serve others under the call God has placed over her life. Kimberly currently resides in South Carolina.

She is a very anointed woman of God who signs, miracles and wonders follow. The miraculous and incessant testimonies attributed to her ministry are incalculable, with many reporting physical and mental healing, financial breakthroughs, debt cancellations and other favorable outcomes. She is known across the globe as a servant who truly labors on behalf of God's people through intercession.

She is the author of The Following:

"Overcoming Difficult Life Experiences with Scriptures and Prayers"
"Overcoming Emotions with Prayers"
"Daily Prayers That Bring Changes"
"In Right Standing,"
"Obedience Is Key,"
"Prayers That Break The Yoke Of The Enemy: A Book Of Declarations,"
"Prayers That Demolish Demonic Strongholds: A Book Of Declarations,"
"Work Smarter. Not Harder. A Book Of Declarations For The Workforce,"
"Set The Captives Free: A Book Of Deliverance."
"Pray More Challenge"
"Walk By Faith: A Daily Devotional"
"Empowering The New Me: Fifty Tips To Becoming A Godly Woman"
"School of the Prophets: A Curriculum For Success"
"8 Keys To Accessing The Supernatural"
"Conquering The Mind: A Daily Devotional"
"Enhancing The Prophetic In You"
"The ABCs of The Prophetic: Prophetic Characteristics"
"Wisdom Is The Principal Thing: A Daily Devotional"
"It Cost Me Everything"

About The Author

"The Making Of A Prophet: Women Walking in Prophetic Destiny"
"The Art of Meditation: A Daily Devotional"
"Warfare Strategies: Biblical Weapons"
"Becoming A Better You"
"I Almost Died"
"The Pastor's Secret: The D.L. Series"
"June Bug The Busy Bee: The Gamer"
"June Bug The Busy Bee: The Bully"
"The Weary Prophet: Providing Practical Steps For Restoration"
"The Insignificant Woman"
"The Foolish Woman: A Daily Devotional"
"June Bug The Busy Bee: Sibling Rivalry"
"All Things Relationships"

You can find more about Kimberly at
www.kimberlyhargraves.com

For Rejoice Essential Magazine, visit
www.rejoiceessential.com

For beauty and t-shirts, visit
www.rejoicingbeauty.com

Please write a review for my books on Amazon.com

Support this ministry:
Cashapp: $ProphetessKimberly
Paypal.me/remag
Venmo: Kimberly-Moses-19

Index

A

a false connection, 46
abandonment, 16, 81, 86, 168
above, 12, 14, 15, 16, 19, 141, 146, 157, 162, 166
abundance, 161
abusive, 19
accomplish, 113, 157
accountability partner, 111
accountable, 7, 75, 94, 125
accusation, 165
accuser of the brethren, 58, 166
achieve, 114
achiever, 113
Adam, 85
addictions, 98
admiration, 50
admire, 67
adultery, 96, 122
adversaries, 145
adversary, 166

adversity, 66, 116
advice, 52, 54, 128, 144
affection, 125
affectionate, 9, 13, 43
affirm, 59, 125
affirmations, 76
afraid, 105, 119, 154
agents of Satan, 30, 86
agitation, 8
alcohol, 98
alcoholic, 133
alignment, 39, 42, 91, 108, 133
ambassador, 140, 147
Amen corner, 76
Amy Cassels, 5
anger, 4, 10, 51, 59, 60, 66, 70, 71, 168
angry, 103
annoyances, 70
anointed, 74, 153, 169
anointing, 32, 94, 143, 149, 153
anxiety, 64, 70, 156
anxiousness, 24, 105, 165
apologize, 102, 103, 131
appreciate, 19, 39, 47, 49, 62, 77, 84, 85, 129, 146
appreciates, 23
arguing, 4, 56, 89
argumentative, 140
arguments, 38, 53, 106, 125
arrogance, 8
arrogant, 19

aspirations, 44
assumptions, 67
atmosphere, 2, 40
attracted, 36, 127
attraction, 78
authority, 4, 33

B

bad, 2, 7, 14, 96, 101
balance, 41, 81
bank, 26, 163
barns, 27
battles, 102, 104, 140, 144
beauty, 35, 171
bed, 3, 7, 56, 73, 88, 129
believe, 7, 9, 82, 90, 98, 120
beloved, 8, 66
beneath, 162
benefits, 18, 23, 26
betrayal, 39, 121
bias, 55
Bible, 90, 92, 135, 167
bills, 159, 160, 161
bind, 8, 10, 11, 14, 15, 16, 18, 19, 20, 21, 24, 25, 26, 27, 28, 32, 33, 36, 37, 38, 39, 41, 42, 43, 44, 47, 49, 50, 53, 57, 58, 64, 69, 70, 71, 72, 77, 81, 84, 86, 87, 89, 97, 98, 99, 100, 101, 105, 117, 119, 121, 122, 124, 125, 126, 129, 130, 132, 134, 139, 141, 145, 147, 154, 156, 157, 161, 163, 164, 165, 166, 168
bipolar disorder, 164

bitterness, 58, 68

blame, 66

bless, 1, 9, 10, 11, 12, 14, 15, 16, 17, 22, 24, 26, 28, 29, 30, 31, 32, 33, 34, 36, 37, 38, 39, 40, 41, 42, 43, 44, 47, 48, 49, 50, 52, 53, 54, 55, 58, 59, 60, 61, 63, 64, 65, 66, 67, 68, 69, 72, 73, 74, 75, 76, 77, 78, 79, 81, 82, 83, 84, 85, 86, 87, 88, 89, 91, 94, 95, 98, 99, 100, 101, 104, 105, 106, 112, 118, 119, 120, 121, 122, 124, 125, 126, 127, 128, 129, 130, 131, 132, 133, 134, 135, 136, 137, 138, 140, 141, 142, 143, 144, 145, 147, 149, 150, 151, 156, 159, 160, 161, 162, 163, 164, 165, 168

blessed, 4, 10, 52, 54, 85, 117, 118, 120, 138, 162

blessing, 3, 9, 20, 23, 64, 74, 76, 80

blessings, 1, 162, 163

blind, 19, 108

blind eye, 19

blocked, 123

blood disorders, 97

bloodline, 99

boastful, 140

body, 17, 53, 62, 63, 71, 96, 97, 99, 100, 101

bold, 29, 110, 151

bond, 1, 35, 36, 42, 46, 48, 82, 85, 125

book, 4

books, 80, 82, 113, 171

borrow, 162

boundaries, 31, 143

boyfriend, 5, 128

breakfast, 7

breakthrough, 5

bride, 68

broken, 38, 44, 46, 71, 89
broom, 29
brother, 133
burden, 23, 31, 82, 91, 133
bush, 27
business, 2, 23, 74, 82, 86

C

calls, 85, 102
cancer, 97
car, 29, 160
care, 15, 28, 29, 51, 74, 131, 146
career-focused, 133
carnal, 90
cash flow, 27
cast out, 3, 4
celebrate, 46, 131
celebration, 81
challenge, 4, 5, 6, 41, 115, 157, 159
challenges, 1, 69, 130
chaos, 3
chaotic, 40
cheat, 31, 124
checkups, 99
cheerful, 87, 105
cheering, 80
cheerleaders, 80
cherish, 62, 123
cherishes, 23

Index

children, 35, 40, 41, 78, 90, 108, 148, 161, 164, 169

chocolates, 23

Christ-like characteristics, 104

church, 13, 68, 92, 109

circumspectly, 116, 144

city, 162

clay, 3

codes, 118

college graduate, 148

combat, 3

comfort, 9, 75, 135, 151

commandments, 135

commendable, 167

commitment, 15, 83

committed, 47, 122, 123, 128, 130

communicate, 51, 53, 56, 57, 60, 62

communication, 36, 51, 53, 57, 59, 60, 64, 84, 89, 109, 121, 127

companion, 85

companionship, 38, 78

company, 35, 85, 130

compassion, 49, 111

compassionate, 8, 21, 66, 139, 146

competition, 77

complaining, 2, 65, 114

compromise, 44, 93, 112, 129

conceit, 10, 20, 139

conceited, 19

conclusions, 67, 168

conduct, 3, 110, 145

confident, 109, 134, 153, 156

conflict, 48, 58, 124
conflict resolution, 48
conquers, 7
conversation, 31, 53
convict, 7
conviction, 2, 43, 152
cook, 18
cooking, 85
corrupt, 60, 112
counsel, 30, 38, 41, 55, 56, 59, 75, 84, 110, 141, 144, 147
counselors, 57
country, 143, 162
couples, 1, 13, 46, 159
courage, 32, 66
courageous, 151
courting, 51, 68
cousins, 148
covenant relationship, 123
covenant-breaking spirits, 16, 42, 77
COVID, 56, 62, 100, 159
creativity, 113
creator, 113
credit scores, 160
crooked path, 117
cross, 76, 98, 151
crucifiers, 4
crucify, 94
cry, 35, 80
Curriculum, 170
cute, 62

D

damage, 99
dancing, 85
dangerous, 99
date, 16, 36, 40, 78, 85, 88, 97
daughter, 133
deaf ear, 53
death, 59, 96
debt, 88, 159, 160, 163, 169
debtors, 163
deception, 165
decisions, 19, 43, 64, 65, 110, 145
declarations, 5
Declarations, 170
declare, 5, 8, 14, 20
decree, 8, 9, 10, 11, 13, 14, 15, 16, 18, 19, 20, 21, 23, 25, 27, 32, 33, 35, 36, 37, 38, 41, 45, 48, 51, 52, 54, 57, 60, 62, 64, 66, 70, 71, 72, 90, 91, 92, 93, 94, 97, 98, 99, 101, 102, 103, 104, 105, 106, 107, 108, 109, 110, 111, 112, 113, 114, 115, 116, 117, 119, 120, 121, 123, 124, 125, 127, 130, 132, 136, 137, 139, 140, 141, 144, 145, 146, 147, 148, 149, 151, 152, 153, 154, 155, 156, 157, 158, 161, 162, 163, 165, 166, 167, 168
dedicate, 64
dedicated, 130, 169
deed, 9, 160
defend, 14, 30, 32, 79
defensive, 140
deleted, 123

delight, 24, 135
deliver, 94, 118, 135, 167
deliverance, 70, 168, 169
delivered, 2, 164
demonic, 3, 28, 32, 48, 57, 58, 68, 72, 89, 90, 99, 119, 134, 135, 165, 166
depression, 101, 157
desire, 12, 41, 56, 96, 113, 129
despise, 116
destiny, 11, 30, 47, 74, 75, 86, 95
destroy, 37, 122, 166
destruction, 21, 138, 145
destructive behaviors, 147
devil, 3, 7, 46, 118, 147, 164, 166, 167
devoted, 2, 15, 16, 141, 144
Devotional, 170, 171
devotions, 92
diabetes, 97
difficulty, 66
dignified, 65
diligent, 25, 115
dimension, 3
dinner time, 108
disagreement, 68
disagreements, 4
disappointment, 50
disappointments, 70, 121
disassociate, 122
discern, 30, 55, 90, 104, 136, 145
discernment, 30, 48, 75, 91, 132

Index

disconnect, 35

disconnected, 46, 86

discord, 82

discouraged, 76

diseases, 32, 96, 101

dismayed, 33

dismiss, 63, 127

disobedient, 19

disrespect, 57

distracted, 44, 53

distractions, 86, 132

divine connections, 46, 151

division, 21, 36, 43, 47, 53, 57, 77, 86, 102, 103, 122

divorce, 42, 57, 89, 128, 159, 164

doctor, 56, 98, 99

domestic violence, 10

doors, 113, 117, 127, 148, 149

double minded, 136

doubts, 121, 124

downs, 1

drama, 38, 57, 102

dreams, 44, 114

drugs, 96

drunk, 99

dry season, 23

dysfunction, 21, 84

E

ears, 54, 144, 147

earth., 151, 166
east, 24
economic crashes, 27
edification, 59
emails, 118
embraced, 96, 164
emotional affairs, 125
emotional baggage, 155
emotionally stable, 111
empathy, 55, 111
encourage, 9, 15, 35, 38, 74, 76, 129
encouraged, 5, 74
encouragement, 32, 74
encourager, 74
endurance, 64
endure, 9, 127
endures, 3
enemies, 33, 38, 106
enemy, 2, 3, 4, 21, 46, 55, 56, 70, 72, 75, 90, 97, 102, 132, 141, 164, 165
engaged, 68
enjoy, 35, 78, 85, 87, 106, 118, 130
entertain, 126, 166
entrepreneur, 169
equally yoked, 90
error, 3
escorted, 29
esteem, 10, 14, 49, 123, 156
evangelist, 93
Eve, 85

everlasting rock, 120
evil, 9, 14, 20, 30, 33, 105, 127, 137
evilness, 32
excellence, 167
excuse making, 25
exercise, 100, 146
exploits, 148
exposed, 4
eye candy, 88
eye contact, 55
eyes, 15, 54, 122, 123, 137, 141, 143, 167

F

faith, 1, 9, 25, 39, 52, 64, 65, 76, 81, 99, 105, 110, 111, 134, 136, 152, 155, 157
faithful, 5, 101, 123, 162
faithfulness, 9, 15, 63
false doctrine, 94
false reality, 168
family, 19, 21, 23, 24, 26, 27, 28, 40, 49, 72, 78, 81, 90, 93, 96, 108, 110, 138, 143, 145, 147, 148, 159, 161
famine, 27
fast, 5, 63, 91, 141, 151
father, 35, 133, 164
fault, 11, 38, 50, 102
fault finding, 11, 38
favor, 2, 5, 26, 115, 149
fear, 25, 29, 89, 93, 119, 140, 141, 144
feelings, 3, 7, 31, 40, 47, 52, 77, 106, 127

fighting, 1, 4, 68, 102
financial attacks, 27
financial strain, 26
fire, 3, 4, 91, 126, 135, 147
flaws, 35, 36, 63, 130
flesh, 7, 18, 87, 94, 107, 119, 137
flint, 34, 116, 151
flirt, 16, 89, 125
flowers, 23
foolish, 49, 104, 138
foolishness, 19, 145
footsteps, 92, 148
forgave, 8
forgive, 68, 69, 71, 72, 163
forgiving, 8, 47, 67, 69, 72
fragmented pieces, 71, 121
fresh air, 76
Friday, 40
friendly, 7
friends, 22, 35, 88, 132, 156
friendship, 49
fruits of the spirit, 9, 63
frustrated, 62
frustrations, 8
fun, 87, 155
fury, 21
future, 5, 52, 117, 136, 164

G

Index

games, 108
gatekeeper, 2
generation, 27, 150
generation curses, 27
generous, 7
gentleness, 9, 139
gift, 3, 85, 112, 117
gifts, 23, 39, 93, 117, 150, 153
glad, 62, 85, 87, 108
globe, 170
glory, 24, 37, 134, 138, 149, 153
gluttonous, 96
gluttony, 97
goals, 44, 113
God, 1, 2, 3, 4, 5, 6, 7, 8, 11, 13, 14, 19, 22, 23, 29, 33, 35, 40, 46, 48, 51, 54, 56, 62, 63, 65, 66, 68, 70, 71, 74, 80, 82, 85, 90, 91, 92, 93, 94, 102, 103, 104, 105, 106, 108, 109, 110, 112, 113, 114, 115, 116, 117, 118, 119, 120, 123, 128, 133, 136, 137, 138, 142, 143, 147, 148, 149, 152, 153, 154, 156, 159, 162, 163, 164, 167, 169, 170
godly, 3, 30, 55, 56, 64, 75, 84, 93, 94, 122, 141, 143, 144
gods, 90
go-getter, 113
good, 3, 4, 9, 14, 21, 26, 27, 37, 40, 51, 63, 64, 85, 94, 97, 105, 114, 117, 137, 143, 145, 154, 162, 167
good judgment, 143
goodness, 9, 63
Goshen, 26
gospel, 93
Gospel of Jesus Christ, 169

gossip, 143
grace, 12, 139
gracious, 60
grateful, 29
great listener, 51, 109
greed, 25
greedy, 19
greener pastures, 25
grieve, 58, 112
grievous, 167
ground beef, 18, 96
ground turkey, 18
grudges, 11, 58, 68, 103
grumbling, 38, 114
guard, 31, 33, 60, 123, 128, 143, 147

H

hair, 62
happy, 20, 80, 108, 123, 130
harm, 28, 30, 152
harmony, 10, 43, 83, 146
harsh, 78, 146
harvest, 106, 163
hastiness, 49
hasty, 66
hate, 29
hatred, 11, 70
head, 108, 162
healing, 11, 60, 98, 118, 169

Index

health, 14, 21, 97, 98, 99, 101

healthy, 28, 48, 72, 83, 96, 100, 101, 131, 146

heart, 1, 3, 11, 16, 31, 43, 49, 50, 52, 54, 63, 66, 70, 71, 90, 92, 93, 94, 97, 104, 106, 111, 118, 119, 128, 129, 131, 134, 137, 138, 139, 140, 142, 147

heartless, 19

Heavenly Father, 166

heavens, 24

height, 29

helper, 27, 157

high blood pressure, 97

high imagination, 71

hindered, 17

hindrance, 101

history, 13

holy, 8, 66, 93

Holy Spirit, 2, 4, 7, 93, 96, 101, 105, 106

home, 2, 4, 19, 21, 29, 39, 40, 42, 57, 58, 74, 80, 89, 101, 102, 108, 123, 160

homosexuality, 96

honest, 45, 63, 109, 124, 129

honey, 11, 26

honor, 1, 11, 16, 78, 83, 121, 124, 128, 133, 139, 140, 162

honorable, 167

honored, 141

hope, 4, 9, 64, 65, 105, 117, 136

hopeful, 76

hospital, 56

hostile, 137

house, 29, 73, 90, 102, 103, 135, 146, 161

household, 9, 26, 52, 102
huffing, 62
hug, 78
humble, 8, 16, 30, 38, 49, 52, 57, 66, 94, 104, 109, 138, 139, 150
humility, 139, 140
hurt, 1, 4, 7, 39, 56, 59, 68, 69, 70, 71, 106, 156
hurtful, 36, 126
husband, 2, 4, 5, 7, 13, 18, 23, 29, 35, 40, 41, 46, 51, 56, 62, 68, 74, 80, 85, 96, 102, 108, 109, 113, 118, 123, 133, 138, 143, 148, 153, 159, 164
hygiene, 100

I

idea, 113
identity, 95
idolatry, 44, 90
imitators, 140
immune system, 100
impart, 75, 144
impatient, 65
impossible, 6
improvement, 2
incompetent, 79
increase, 24, 49, 54, 87, 143, 150, 160
infidelity, 4, 42
infirmities, 98
influence, 3, 58, 72, 99, 134, 149
information, 51, 122, 154
in-laws, 31, 41

Index

innovative, 109, 149
insecure, 118
insecurities, 70, 118, 124
insecurity, 37, 81, 154
insensitive, 106
insomnia, 100
inspiration, 75, 149
inspire, 83
instability, 47
instructed, 2
instructions, 52
integrity, 109, 122, 161
intercede, 2
intercession, 5, 91, 133, 170
intercessor, 2, 169
interest, 10, 18, 42, 51, 78
intimacy, 48, 87, 125
invest, 36, 40, 41, 83, 85, 88, 91, 131, 146
investing, 80
invisible, 80, 154
irritate, 1
issues, 2, 58, 155, 166

J

jealous, 154
jealousy, 10, 14, 37, 70, 81, 121
Jesus, 2, 4, 8, 9, 10, 11, 12, 13, 14, 15, 16, 18, 19, 20, 21, 22, 23, 24, 25, 26, 27, 28, 30, 31, 32, 33, 34, 35, 36, 37, 38, 39, 41, 42, 43, 44, 45, 46, 47, 48, 49, 50, 51, 53, 54, 55, 57, 58, 59, 64, 68,

69, 70, 71, 72, 75, 76, 77, 78, 80, 81, 82, 83, 84, 86, 89, 91, 92, 95, 97, 98, 99, 100, 101, 102, 103, 104, 105, 106, 109, 110, 111, 112, 113, 114, 115, 116, 119, 121, 122, 123, 124, 125, 126, 127, 129, 130, 131, 132, 134, 135, 136, 138, 139, 140, 141, 142, 145, 146, 147, 148, 149, 153, 154, 155, 156, 157, 160, 161, 163, 164, 165, 166, 167, 168, 169

Jesus Christ, 4, 33, 78, 91, 95, 102, 105, 110, 124, 134, 140, 147, 153, 154, 165, 169

job, 2, 23, 26, 28, 101

joke, 62, 68

journal, 2

joy, 9, 63, 64, 76, 85, 105

judgmental, 49, 72

June Bug, 171

just, 8, 62, 74, 93, 128, 167

K

kids, 41

Kimberly Hargraves, 169

Kimberly Moses, 169

kind, 7, 8, 9, 11, 13, 66, 72, 130

Kindness, 7

King Solomon, 90

Kingdom, 2, 16, 26, 44, 50, 71, 89, 90, 91, 133

Kings, 39, 90

kiss, 78

knowledge, 144, 165

knowledgeable, 143

L

labor, 37
land, 26, 117, 160, 162
laugh, 68, 87
law, 50, 106
lazy, 25, 114
leader, 108, 147
leadership, 19, 94, 108, 112
leaves, 120
legal fees, 159
leisure time, 85
lies, 3, 121, 164
lifestyle, 96, 100
lifetime, 20
lion of Judah, 151
lips, 60
listen, 44, 52, 55, 59, 108, 141, 164
loneliness, 43, 81, 86
Loneliness, 85
lonely, 3
Lord, 1, 2, 3, 5, 7, 9, 10, 11, 12, 14, 15, 16, 17, 21, 22, 24, 25, 26, 27, 28, 29, 30, 31, 32, 33, 34, 36, 37, 38, 39, 40, 41, 42, 43, 44, 45, 47, 48, 49, 50, 52, 53, 54, 55, 57, 58, 59, 60, 61, 63, 64, 65, 66, 67, 69, 71, 72, 73, 74, 75, 76, 77, 78, 79, 80, 81, 82, 83, 84, 85, 86, 87, 88, 89, 91, 92, 93, 94, 95, 97, 98, 99, 100, 101, 102, 104, 105, 106, 111, 112, 113, 115, 116, 117, 118, 119, 120, 121, 122, 124, 125, 126, 127, 128, 129, 130, 131, 132, 133, 134, 135, 136, 137, 138, 139, 140, 141, 142, 143, 144, 145, 147, 149, 150,

151, 152, 153, 154, 156, 157, 158, 159, 160, 161, 162, 163, 164, 165, 166, 167, 168

love, 1, 3, 7, 9, 10, 13, 14, 15, 16, 17, 18, 19, 23, 25, 35, 36, 37, 39, 40, 42, 43, 46, 49, 51, 54, 57, 60, 62, 63, 68, 69, 78, 83, 89, 92, 93, 101, 106, 109, 110, 119, 124, 128, 130, 133, 134, 137, 139, 161, 167

lovely, 167

lover, 19

loving, 1, 3, 13, 16, 59, 65, 106, 125, 130, 146, 169

loyal, 123, 128

lust, 21, 107, 122

M

mad, 68, 123, 128

malice, 60, 103

manipulation, 20, 41

manipulative tactics, 1

marital vows, 124, 128

marriage, 1, 2, 3, 4, 5, 13, 15, 16, 18, 19, 20, 23, 26, 32, 36, 37, 38, 39, 40, 41, 42, 43, 44, 47, 48, 49, 50, 51, 61, 66, 68, 69, 70, 71, 72, 74, 77, 82, 83, 84, 85, 86, 87, 88, 89, 118, 119, 121, 122, 123, 124, 125, 126, 127, 130, 131, 132, 133, 138, 143, 145,146, 154, 155, 156, 159, 166

married, 1, 5, 23, 46, 48, 108, 123, 126, 143, 157, 169

marry, 96

mate, 3

media projects, 153

medical bills, 159

meditate, 136, 167

meek, 8, 66, 140

meekness, 139, 145

memories, 36, 79, 87, 124

mental trauma, 70

mentor, 169

merciful, 12

messages, 35, 123

Metrice Coleman Wilder, 5

mind, 92, 103, 104, 105, 118, 134, 136, 137, 147, 164, 165, 166, 167

mindful, 37

minister, 2

ministry, 29, 40, 73, 74, 75, 80, 82, 86, 169, 171

miracles, 135, 169

miraculous, 169

miscommunication, 36, 53, 57

misses, 85

mistake, 1

mistakes, 48, 68, 77, 138, 143

mistreatment, 21, 72

misunderstandings, 48

Monday, 40

money, 13, 24, 25, 26, 159, 161, 163

mother, 133, 169

motivate, 39, 75, 109, 149

motive, 1, 123

motives, 20, 21, 30, 126, 130

mourning, 85

mouths, 8, 58, 60, 142

multimedia, 113

multitude, 14, 55, 57, 69, 131

N

Nabal, 138
narcissistic behavior, 20
nations, 162, 169
negative words, 59
negativity, 84
neglect, 37, 41, 81, 94, 129
negligent, 99
nerves, 56
new creature, 166
new creatures, 133
noon prayer, 4
north, 24
nutrients, 100

O

obedient, 92, 117
obeyed, 5, 7
obscene talk, 60
offended, 3, 56, 59
offense, 68, 69, 127
offenses, 38
oil, 26
open Heaven, 114
opinion, 55
opposition, 66

optimistic, 76, 111, 166
Overcoming, 170
overflow, 26, 114, 161
overlooked, 9
overwhelm, 78, 156

P

pain, 11, 65, 70, 97
pandemic, 62, 159
paranoid, 166
parents, 19
partners, 22, 46
partnership, 49
passion, 36, 74, 126, 132, 156
passionate, 78
passwords, 118, 122, 154
patience, 9, 62, 63, 64, 65, 139
patient, 3, 8, 13, 16, 50, 51, 59, 62, 63, 64, 65, 66, 145
peace, 9, 28, 32, 57, 63, 78, 89, 102, 104, 105, 106, 120, 165
peaceful, 40
peacemakers, 102
perseverance, 116
personality, 111
photographer, 148
photography, 74, 113, 153
photoshoots, 74
pioneer, 148
plague, 100
plagues, 33

plans, 45, 115, 117, 119, 127, 164
plenty, 27
pocket, 24
pockets, 160
poor, 9
porch, 29
positive, 74, 76, 88
potato chips, 96
potter, 3
poverty, 14, 163
power, 20, 64, 105, 135, 148, 150, 153
powerful, 4, 90
praise worthy, 167
praised, 141
pray, 1, 2, 3, 4, 5, 10, 11, 12, 19, 20, 21, 22, 24, 25, 27, 28, 41, 42, 44, 45, 46, 47, 48, 49, 52, 53, 54, 55, 56, 58, 59, 60, 63, 64, 65, 71, 75, 77, 78, 79, 80, 85, 86, 87, 88, 89, 90, 91, 92, 94, 99, 110, 117, 124, 125, 126, 127, 129, 137, 138, 139, 140, 141, 142, 143, 150, 151, 157, 165, 167
prayer, 1, 2, 3, 4, 5, 7, 31, 54, 64, 91, 99, 120, 133, 144, 156
Prayers, 170
preach, 80, 93
preaching, 13, 80
premature death, 33, 99
pride, 3, 41, 57, 138
priesthood, 108
prioritize, 135
priority, 40, 81, 124
problem solver, 150
problems, 72, 73, 88, 159

Index

problem-solving, 109
procrastination, 25
procrastinator, 114
productive, 111
products, 82
profit, 115
prolific author, 169
promises, 6, 16, 63, 81, 120, 156
promoted, 80, 141
promotion, 24
property, 160
prophecies, 116, 136, 151
prophecy, 13
prophet, 2, 56
prophetic, 47, 75, 169
prophetic insight, 47
prosper, 1, 13, 24, 33, 65, 66, 114, 115, 150, 164
prosperous, 167
protect, 29, 30, 31, 32, 100, 152
protecting, 1, 3
protection, 4, 32, 121, 130
protects, 2
proud, 19, 76, 82, 139
provider, 23
puffing, 62
punish, 87
punishment, 72, 90, 119
pure, 20, 112, 128, 137, 147, 167
purity, 110, 139, 167
purpose, 11, 30, 37, 59, 75, 80, 86, 95, 149

Q

quality time, 107
Queens, 39
questions, 5
quiet time, 64

R

ram, 27
ramen noodles, 96
realistic expectations, 48
reap, 64, 106, 163
rebellion, 41
receptive, 71
reciprocated, 11
reckless, 19, 44
recognition, 81
reconciliation, 73
recover, 91
refute, 145
regenerate, 99
rejection, 50
rejoice, 8, 63, 64, 141
Rejoice Essential Magazine, 171
relationships, 1, 15, 30, 46, 68, 127, 155
renew, 60, 103, 126, 136, 147, 164, 165
repent, 59, 140
repented, 2, 56

reputation, 29, 31
reschedule, 45
research, 114
resentfulness, 8
resentment, 50, 70
resourceful, 116
respect, 5, 32, 42, 50, 56, 79, 83, 106, 121, 124, 129, 133
respected, 109
respectful, 67, 129
restlessness, 105
restore, 46, 71, 99, 110, 121
retaliate, 7
retirement package, 26
retribution, 71
revelation, 17, 151
revenge, 11, 71
reverence, 16
Rhema word, 151
rich, 25, 115, 161, 163
riches, 14, 24, 161, 163
righteous, 54
righteousness, 11, 44, 106, 110, 142, 162
risky, 96, 99
rivalry, 10, 20, 139
roaring lion, 166
romantic gestures, 129
rough place, 117
royalty, 31
rude, 7
rudeness, 8

S

sabotage, 21, 141, 145, 168
sacrifice, 82, 136
safe, 29, 102
salt, 60, 151
saltiness, 151
sanctified, 91
satisfied, 19
saved, 90, 91, 133
scalp, 29
scandals, 32, 112
schizophrenia, 164
scorned, 133
seared conscience, 94
season, 66, 80, 104, 137, 159, 162
secrets, 15, 35, 72, 77, 118, 122, 154
secure, 29, 52
security, 120
seductress, 15, 122
self-centered, 1, 133
self-control, 63, 168
self-controlled, 65
self-discipline, 111
selfish, 10, 16, 18, 21, 87, 96, 130, 145
selfishness, 43, 47, 139
separation, 57, 89
servant, 3, 111, 140, 170
serve, 2, 3, 5, 10, 43, 131, 169

Index

services, 82
serving, 1, 18, 90
sex, 31, 131, 143
sexual problems, 72
sexually, 32, 101
shame, 52, 115, 139
sharpened, 93
sheep, 54
Shepherd, 24
shield, 115, 122, 145
shortcomings, 84
siblings, 41
sick, 56, 91, 96
sickness, 14, 68, 69, 70, 98, 99, 101, 131
significant, 10, 20, 42, 139
signs, 135, 169
silent, 78, 144
single mentality, 19, 87, 124
single's mentality, 10
sins, 14, 68, 69, 131
sister, 133
skin disorders, 97
slander, 60
slanderous,, 19
sleep, 7, 88, 105, 129
slothful spirit, 25
small beginnings, 116
smile, 20
sober minded, 166
sober-minded, 65

social media, 29, 123
social skills, 111
society, 9, 101
sofa, 5
soft answer, 60
son, 102, 133
sons of Issachar, 117
soul, 11, 70, 92, 97, 110, 118, 167
soulish realm, 164
sound mind, 10, 110, 165
south, 24
spirit of betrayal, 70
spirit of excellence, 94
spirit of retaliation, 21, 71
spiritual call, 47
spiritual connection, 90
spiritual growth, 91
spiritually, 5, 84, 86, 91
spoil, 83
spouse, 1, 2, 3, 4, 5, 8, 9, 10, 11, 12, 13, 14, 15, 16, 17, 18, 19, 20, 21, 22, 23, 24, 25, 26, 27, 28, 29, 30, 31, 32, 33, 34, 35, 36, 37, 38, 39, 40, 41, 42, 43, 44, 45, 46, 47, 48, 49, 50, 51, 52, 53, 54, 55, 56, 57, 58, 59, 60, 61, 62, 63, 64, 65, 66, 67, 68, 69, 70, 71, 72, 73, 74, 75, 76, 77, 78, 79, 80, 81, 82, 83, 84, 85, 86, 87, 88, 89, 90, 91, 92, 93, 94, 95, 97, 98, 99, 100, 101, 102, 103, 104, 105, 106, 107, 108, 109, 110, 111, 112, 113, 114, 115, 116, 117, 118, 119, 120, 121, 122, 123, 124, 125, 126, 127, 128, 129, 130, 131, 132, 133, 134, 135, 136, 137, 138, 139, 140, 141, 142, 143, 144, 145, 146, 147, 148, 149, 150, 151, 152, 153, 154, 155, 156, 157, 158, 159, 160, 161, 162, 163, 164, 165, 166, 167, 168

Index

starve, 18
steadfast, 66, 119
steward, 3, 26, 94, 137
stinginess, 21
store, 62
storm, 35, 54, 90, 138
strangers, 73
strategies, 149, 160
strategy, 159
stray dog, 29
streams of income, 150
strength, 7, 29, 30, 43, 76, 85, 120
stress, 32, 64, 70, 125, 156, 161
strife, 10, 21, 36, 47, 53, 57, 102, 103
strokes, 97
strongholds, 68, 99, 135, 167
stubborn, 56, 98, 139
stubborn,, 56
stubbornness, 3
student loans, 159, 160
study, 94
stumble, 12, 55, 106, 132
stupid, 79
submit, 16, 43, 83, 94, 108, 129, 167
successful, 47, 125
suffer, 1, 90
supernatural, 23, 24, 153, 159
Supernatural, 170
supply, 24, 163
support, 46, 48, 50, 78, 80, 83, 84, 160

supporter, 81
supportive, 111
surprises, 23
surrendered, 138
sweet nothings, 125
sympathy, 9
synergy, 131

T

table, 18, 23, 108
tail, 162
tally marks, 2
tastes, 18
taxes, 160
teachable, 112, 138, 143
teachable spirit, 112, 138
teaching, 8
team, 22, 43, 46, 82, 125, 129, 148
Team Moses, 46
tech-savvy, 111
temperance, 9
temptation, 15, 132, 155
tenderhearted, 8, 72
tenderness, 31
texts, 4, 85
thick, 1, 14, 48
thin, 1, 14, 48
thirty, 2, 4, 98
thoughtful, 67

Index

thoughts, 62, 126, 166
threat, 90, 123
threefold cord, 38
threshold, 2
throats, 56
Tiara Figueroa, 5
time management, 111, 150
time management skills, 111, 150
toil, 115
tongues, 8
touch, 78, 114
tough, 1, 23, 66, 115
towel, 2
toxic people, 155
tragedies, 32, 100
trailblazer, 148
transform, 3, 138
transformed, 2, 133, 134, 136, 165
transition, 131
traumatic experiences, 167
travel, 88
traveling, 85, 159
treacherous, 19
trends, 148
trials, 36, 65, 74, 76
tribulation, 63, 64
tribulations, 76
Tron, 13, 169
troubled, 104
true, 121, 164, 167

trust, 7, 36, 48, 56, 65, 71, 77, 105, 118, 119, 120, 121, 140, 141, 150, 154, 166

trustworthy, 112

truth, 8, 9, 56, 58, 60, 93, 168

truthful, 146

tumors, 97

tv, 5

U

understand, 46, 47, 49, 89

understanding, 44, 46, 50, 52, 104, 119

unemployment, 27

unequally yoked, 90

unforgiveness, 38, 58, 69, 70, 72, 106, 131

unfriended, 123

ungrateful, 19

ungratefulness, 77

unhealthiness, 96

unholy, 19

unify, 35

uniqueness, 49

unity, 49, 57, 131

unrighteousness, 21

unshakeable, 124

unwilling, 18

ups, 1

upset, 5, 59, 68, 71, 87

V

vain imagination, 126
vats, 27
victorious, 157
videos, 80
vigilant, 166
vindicate, 33
vision, 46, 82, 113
visionary, 109
vitamins, 100
vlog, 46
voice, 52, 54, 55, 58, 92, 149, 169
vow, 1

W

wandering eyes, 15, 42
warfare, 74, 102
Warfare Strategies, 171
warlocks, 30
water, 120
wealth, 150, 161, 162
wealthy, 27
weapon, 33, 115
weary, 64, 116
weekends, 40
west, 24
whisper, 125, 165
wicked, 65
widow, 56

wife, 2, 13, 18, 41, 68, 85, 108, 109, 133

wilderness, 23, 159

win, 2, 3, 149

wine, 27

wisdom, 8, 26, 31, 47, 52, 53, 60, 75, 84, 104, 117, 137, 140, 143, 144, 145

wise, 54, 137, 141, 143, 144, 145

witchcraft, 1, 20, 42

witches, 30

woman, 2, 138, 169

womanizer, 133

wonders, 135, 169

words of knowledge, 52

work injuries, 101

world, 40, 136, 151, 155, 165, 169

worried, 7, 103

worship, 93, 94

wrath, 21, 49, 58, 60, 73, 103, 128

wrestling, 4

writing, 153

wrongdoing, 8, 33, 126

Y

yield, 43, 70, 104, 168

yielded, 140

Z

zealous, 91, 116